CHARACTER *in* LITERATURE

Also by Baruch Hochman

*Another Ego: Self and Society in the
  Work of D. H. Lawrence*
The Fiction of S. Y. Agnon
*The Test of Character: From the
  Victorian Novel to the Modern*

CHARACTER *in* LITERATURE

Baruch Hochman

Cornell University Press

ITHACA AND LONDON

International Standard Book Number 0-8014-1787-2
Library of Congress Catalog Card Number 84–45809
Printed in the United States of America
*Librarians: Library of Congress cataloging information
appears on the last page of the book.*

*The paper in this book is acid-free and meets the guidelines for
permanence and durability of the Committee on Production Guidelines
for Book Longevity of the Council on Library Resources.*

Contents

Preface

The issue of character in literature has been with me for a long time. I have always assumed, with Wordsworth, that the poet is a man speaking to men and that literature is a prism through which we confront ourselves and our world. I have therefore been pained, even when I have been exhilarated, by the mounting impulse to discount the human element in literature. I have been pained because the substance of literature is dissipated if we pretend that characters have nothing to do with people; I have been exhilarated by the elegance of the strategies and structures that recent schools of reading have disclosed.

This book grows out of that pain and that exhilaration. I believe that characters in literature have more in common with people in life than contemporary critical discourse suggests. What they have in common is the model, which we carry in our heads, of what a person is. Both characters and people are apprehended in someone's consciousness, and they are apprehended in approximately the same terms. Yet they are clearly not identical. To equate them is to overlook the peculiarities of their habitation—which for characters in literature is the world of language—and to erode the salient qualities of both characters themselves and the texts that generate them.

In the pages that follow I tread a delicate line between the view that readers must apprehend a character in their own terms and the view that readers must honor the terms laid down by a text. I hope I keep a reasonable balance as I move along that line.

I also hope that readers can accept one major limitation in the scope of my discussion. I have limited myself to figures that are directly presented as characters—on the whole, those that are named, that are endowed with traits, and that "ask" us to envision them, for a moment at least, on the model of people. I have not dealt with other figures or voices inscribed in texts. Originally, I had meant to deal with such figures and voices. I had intended to blur traditional distinctions between narrative, drama, and lyric poetry. Since speech implies a speaker, literary speech suggests to us the character of the speaker, whether that speaker is the narrator of *Tom Jones* or the voice that "utters" a lyric poem. This is so whether we call the speaker "the author" or "the implied author" or the "sound" aspect of the per*sona* or any identifiable dimension of the language from which a patch of discourse is woven. But to have taken on voices as well as figures would have involved formidable difficulties in a book of this length. As a result, my own discourse here deals only with those entities that we conventionally call characters, as they figure in what I have called the "surface structure" of the text—that is, its manifest "world" of actions and agents. Clearly the term *surface structure*, in the context of current critical discourse, is a controversial choice, but it seems to me the simplest way to say what I mean. I hope my readers will grant me my meaning here, as elsewhere, since my aim has been not to engage all of the issues that arise in the course of this study but to hew out a view of character that may be useful to readers, whatever their critical persuasion.

Many friends helped to make this book what it is.

Martin Green, Ilja Wachs, and my wife, Barbara, read an early draft and confirmed that it existed; as always, Barbara went on reading, magnanimously, through many revisions.

Shimon Sandbank read generously, with eagle eye and ready mind. Ruth Nevo pinpointed a crucial issue in the manuscript. Morton Bloomfield scouted material all along the way and offered perspective-yielding wisdom on what I came to write.

Then there were those who struck sparks of wisdom or doubt with a word, a glance, a challenge: Leon Balter, Anita Mittwoch, Shlomith Rimmon-Kenan, Arthur Klein, Elizabeth Freund, Violet Khazoum, Josh Adler, Jona Rosenfeld, Don Shapiro, Tamara Green, and Herbert and Judith Weil. Thanks are due to them all.

I thank, too, the students with whom, over the past seven years, I threshed out much of what came to be this book; the members of the Staff Seminar of the English Department of the Hebrew University, on whom I tried out one of the chapters and who will recognize some of their views in its pages; the Hebrew University, with whose financial support I wrote, in 1981–82, a part of what figures here; and Judy Friedgut, Doron Narkiss, Emily Shapiro, Jackie Stein, and Eva Vilarrubí, as well as editors at Cornell University Press (especially Christie Lerch and Marilyn M. Sale), for generous help in preparing the manuscript for publication. Bernhard Kendler was most kind in facilitating publication of the book.

BARUCH HOCHMAN

Jerusalem

CHARACTER *in* LITERATURE

I

The Case against Character

Character has not fared well in our century. In the world of action, mass society has flattened our sense of the salience of character and even of its relevance. In the world of thought, a pride of powerful doctrines has eroded our sense of its quiddity, its stability, and even its reality. The notion of the unconscious, for example—whether conceived in Freudian, Marxist, or Durkheimian terms—has vitiated our notion of character as a thing of substance. So have the scientific and pseudoscientific ideas that haunt our thinking, not to speak of the technologies that order our lives and subordinate people to other urgencies. Literature reflects life with regard to character as in other respects. Even where writers have bucked prevailing creeds, their work has served as the vehicle for a growing skepticism about the reality of character. Hence its progressive attenuation as a recognized element in literary texts. Over the past fifty years the characters of literature have, in the works of our most innovative writers, often been reduced to schematic angularity, vapid ordinariness, or allegorical inanity. The great writers of early modernism fulfilled the Romantic program of individualism and created a gallery of unprecedentedly complex characters, but their heirs have deliberately subordinated the role of character in their work. And they have done so with the conviction that neither life nor literature can effectively accommodate rich, full-bodied, interesting, and sustained manifestations of character—of embodied human being or viable personal identity.[1]

If Samuel Beckett, for example, has a vital theme beyond the blabbification of language, it is the emptying out of the self and the loss of its meaning.[2] And if postmodernism has a range of bugaboos that it attacks as fictive, character as a substantial reality is not the least of them. Postmodernist writers not only challenge the cogency of character as a category but actively work to dismantle it as an operative element in their stories. Nabokov is a prime example of this tendency, but virtually all of the innovative writers of the past forty or fifty years have participated in it. Such writers include both those who openly denigrate character and those who seem to embrace it. Such writers range from Bellow to Borges, from Solzhenitsyn to Pynchon, from Camus and Sartre to Sarraute and Robbe-Grillet.[3]

Literary theorists, literary critics, and literary scholars have collaborated with the novelists, playwrights, and poets in subordinating character to other elements in literature. As early as 1965, John Harvey, in *Character and the Novel*— probably the best twentieth-century study of character in literature to date—copiously documented the extent to which modern letters have denigrated character as a component of literature.[4] Surveying the modernist achievement in the creation of character, Harvey also pinpointed the grounds of the case against character in twentieth-century critical and creative traditions.

The case against character has been made from a great many vantage points: textual, historical, literary-critical, ideological, metaphysical, and theoretical. Critics belonging to the most traditional schools of literary scholarship, as well as writers identified with the antitraditional extremes of deconstructionism, have joined in the ritual of cannibalization. At the extreme left, a radical case is made against the values of post-Renaissance individualism and against the disposition to create and interpret character in terms of it. This view, held by some structuralists and many post-structuralists, insists that the "privileging" of character reflects a distorting bourgeois bias that stresses individuals and their choices rather than the world they live in.[5] On the far right, conservative scholars affirm a rigorous historicism that restricts the reading of texts, and of the characters in them, to the terms of discourse appropriate to the times and genres that generated them. For such scholars it is foolish to ponder the motives of a Shylock, a Falstaff, or a Hamlet. Only consciousness of the stylized Renaissance conventions for rendering a villain, a satanic tempter, or a revenge hero can help to make sense of such a character, since what we are talking about is not a person and therefore cannot have the consistency or the inwardness of a person. A still more radical historicism, confronting more archaic texts such as Homer's epics, holds that we cannot conceptualize unified images of characters in certain texts because the language of the texts contains no conception of a unified person.[6]

The main burden of the assault on character has rested, however, on more radical approaches to literary criticism that have tended to wrench literature from its historical contexts and to stress only its "literariness." Chief among these are the New Criticism in England and America and structuralism in France, both of which cut literature off from life (and therefore from history) with varying degrees of rigor. Because of their centrality in defining the issues in the case, both seem worth examining in some detail.

From the beginning, the New Criticism took a dim view of character. The New Critics not only banished poetry's chief protagonist—the poet—from poetry but also insisted that imaginary people were not relevant to literature. G. Wilson Knight expressed a characteristic view when he argued, in *The Wheel of Fire* (1928), that if we focus on the characters in Shakespearean tragedy, we distort the plays by introducing considerations of morality into works of art that ideally are structures of imagery existing beyond good and evil. What matters, according to Wilson Knight, is the vision of life conveyed by the imagery of the work.[7] In his view, thinking about people in texts, instead of image patterns, leads us to worry about the characters' ethical nature and to judge them, rather than to contemplate the emerging structure of meanings in the play.[8] L. C. Knights, in "How Many Children Had Lady Macbeth?" (1934), insisted on an analogous point: that any concern with Lady Macbeth's character or with biographical issues such as the question of how many children she had is absurd, since the life of the play lies not in the characters or their lives but in the language of the play and the structure of the imagery.[9]

The title of Knights's article—more telling and more vividly remembered by most readers than his argument—reflected the prevailing discontent with Romantic and post-Romantic emphasis on character as such. The Romantic interest in personality, individuality, and originality had directed the attention of nineteenth-century readers to the characters of literature and their motivation. More than that: Enchanted with the impression of life that certain characters in literature gave, the Romantics and post-Romantics often spoke of these figures as though they had really lived, and critics felt free to discuss dimensions of the characters' experience that went well beyond the boundaries of the works in which they appeared. Hence, at a vulgar level, critics (or fantasts) set out to investigate the childhood of Shakespeare's heroines or to consider the question, arising from ambiguities in the text, of how many children Lady Macbeth had, or the effect of the sixteenth-century curriculum at the University of Wittenberg on Hamlet's character. At a somewhat more sophisticated level, Samuel Butler, speaking of Hamlet, Don Quixote, Mr. Pickwick, and others, insisted that "the great characters live as truly as the memory of dead men. For the life after death, it is not necessary that a man or woman have lived."[10] Not having lived, a character could nonetheless be subject, in the view of such readers, to the kind of investigation of motives that people are subject to. Thus Ernest Jones, in considering

Hamlet's motives, in *Hamlet and Oedipus* (1949), generalized that "no dramatic criticism of the personae in the play is possible except under the pretence that they are living persons . . . [we must] inquire what manner of man such a person must have been to feel and act . . . [as] Shakespeare tells us he did."[11] Jones's psychoanalytic reading is formulated within a conception of Shakespeare's heroes as people that received its most eloquent formulation in A. C. Bradley's *Shakespearean Tragedy* (1904).[12]

Knight, Knights, and the New Critics were reacting against these conceptions, as were such historicist scholars as E. E. Stoll and Bruno Snell. All of these writers recoiled from the tendency to confuse literature and life—to contaminate the pristine quality of the literary artifact with the muck and moil of life. In effect, the New Critics and their contemporaries were formulating a view of character and its relationship to literature which was linked to the one that T. S. Eliot formulated in "Tradition and the Individual Talent"—the idea that the poet does not express himself or his own personality but only the inherent possibilities of poetry.[13] The emphasis, according to Eliot, should be not on the poet or on the poet's feeling and thought but on the field of cultural and linguistic reference that constitutes "tradition." Poetry—not passion, personality, or life—was to be the center of interest. Personae could be defined, Yeatsian "masks" assumed, and dramatic voices projected, but coherent simulacra of people were not to be extrapolated from poetry and envisioned as entities in themselves, and their implications were not to be seriously entertained. Crazy Jane and the Bishop, much like William Blake's nurses in his *Songs*, were to be conceived as attitudes or moral stances, not as representations of people. So were full-blown characters in plays and stories.

The prejudice was for literature and against life; for literariness and against personality. It was in effect a prejudice against the self, the soul, the individual—against character as a relatively autonomous component of the literary text. The text and the play of elements within it were to be studied, and no special interest or attention was to be paid to the people engendered by the text and operative within it. If character was to be spoken of at all, it was to be grasped as a more or less irrelevant figment of the reader's imagination, inimical to adequate perception of the work in which it figures. Thus, in the sharpest formulation of this view that we have within the New Critical tradition, C. H. Rickword, in "A Note on Fiction" (1930), insisted that "character is merely the term by which the reader alludes to the pseudo-objective images he composes of his response to an author's verbal arrangements."[14] Hence the problem. "Only as precipitates from the memory are plot and character tangible, yet only in solution has either any emotive value."[15] O. B. Hardison (1968) went still further, in his commentary on Aristotle's *Poetics*, insisting that characters, as agents of the author's intentions, cannot be motivated at all. In his view, only the author has motives; characters merely enact the deeds projected by their creators as part of the governing design.[16]

Within the New Critical–formalist tradition, recent scholars have again taken up the long-neglected issues concerning character and have begun to press them to the breaking point. Ironically, this has happened because they have tried to approach the issues with greater interest and sympathy than their forebears. Unlike Wilson Knight and L. C. Knights, Martin Price and Rawdon Wilson confront the question of character from a posture of affirmation. They strive not to subordinate it to other elements in the text but to find appropriate terms of discourse for dealing with it. "My objective," writes Martin Price in "The Other Self: Thoughts about Character in the Novel" (1968), "is to recover more clearly the inevitable artifice in the conception of character. The character we admire as the result of long attention is something constructed by conventions as arbitrary as any other, and we can only hope to recover an art by recognizing it as art."[17] "On Character: A Reply to Martin Price" (1975),

Rawdon Wilson, who welcomes Price's view only to argue with him in the end, goes still further. Wilson insists axiomatically that "the distinction between characters and real persons is absolute," so that we must ask different questions about characters in fiction than about people in life.[18]

The great strength, and the great difficulty, of Price's and Wilson's position is their heightening of the issue of the relationship between life and art. Their view, as I shall try to show, is ultimately not viable because of the gulf they see between the questions we ask about characters in fiction and the questions we ask about people in life. Indeed, in Wilson's more recent treatment of the problem (1979), he implicitly backs away from his demand for an absolute distinction between character in literature and people in life and proposes that we view conflict of values as the ground of character creation and character retrieval, or as the "constitutive element" of character. Beyond that, explicitly siding with John Harvey, Wilson insists that the purpose of character creation is the engagement of our imagination with the moral issues implicit in human behavior: that is, with the very things that engage us when we talk about human behavior in life.[19]

There is great honesty in Wilson's position, and still more in his shifts of position. The radical dichotomy between art and life does not hold up, except as a strategy for elucidating the ways in which art works, and such elucidation, as Wilson finally shows, tends to reduce itself to arid studies of artifice. It is no accident that the New Critical position ends up in Wilson's impasse. The New Critical view, despite its insistence on the autonomous nature of the literary artifact, is a radically thematizing approach, and thematization always implies a particular life orientation.[20] That is, thematization may be said to reflect a concern with the way in which texts are organized so as to refer to issues in life. Indeed, Wilson's trajectory in his discussion of character so far has in effect reenacted the essential tension in the New Critical position, the tension that has led him first to

insist on the absolute difference between character in literature and character in life and then to insist on the essential
congruity between them in the field of moral interest.

The kinds of difficulty that Wilson has encountered do
not beset the structuralists and post-structuralists, who avoid
it, not by insisting primarily on the absolute literariness of
character in fiction or drama but by insisting on the utter
subordination of character to narrative, and—in the more
radical versions—to what they call text. In doing this, they
go far beyond, say, Wilson Knight. Knight merely subordinates character to a reading of the thematic patterns of a
work, so that character and our reading of it become a
vehicle for thematic material. This is what happens in Knight's
eccentric reading of *Hamlet*, where, to vindicate his reversal
of values in the play, he must read Hamlet as evil and
Claudius as good.[21] Structuralists avoid such reversions to
issues of character by more or less steady reliance on the
notion of character as a function of narrative structure, a
notion that springs from the seminal work of Vladimir
Propp.

Propp, whose *Morphology of the Folk Tale* was published in
1928, propounded the dramatic—and credible—idea that the
characters who people the Russian folktale are of no interest
in themselves. What is central is the story, which can be seen
to have a determinate structure of events within which the
characters operate as functions of the action. As in Aristotle's
view of tragedy, but far more radically, in Propp's theory the
characters are seen as agents of the plot, as secondary elements necessary to the enactment of the story. In the folktale,
according to Propp, the functional, facilitating aspect of
character is so radical as to permit the interchangeability of
agents. What matters, for example, is that the hero vanquish
his enemy, not who the enemy is, or who—a bear, an old
woman, a princess—gives him the winged horse, the magic
ring, or the enchanted spear. The stories are not written to

focus our attention on the characters, and they give us no grounds for contemplating the characters in and for themselves.[22]

Although Propp was concerned only with the folktale, and only with the Russian folktale at that, he has been the mainstay of the structuralist-formalist view of character. In effect he provided a conception that made it possible to neutralize what Tzvetan Todorov called the "privileged" status of character in fiction.[23] For Henry James, who represents the culmination of an older tradition, character and action were the twin pillars of narrative, sustaining each other; for Todorov and Barthes, character is a wholly subordinate element. In a famous question, James, speaking in the spirit of the novel but also of the major forms of Western drama, asked, "What is character but the determination of incident? What is incident but the illustration of character?"[24] The structuralists in effect ask, "What is incident but the substance of narrative?" In James's conception of fiction, character is a substantive entity, present within the text and sufficiently embodied to be revealed in the manifold network of its motivations. For the structuralists, character is there to carry forward the action or (for the less radical) to amplify the theme.

James, like the structuralists, was expressing a prejudice, but also a judgment and a conception of literature. We cannot read *The Portrait of a Lady* wholly in terms of James's statement, in the preface, that the kernel out of which the book grew came to him in the image of a person, of "a young woman affronting her destiny."[25] Yet if we look at the novel as written, it seems very likely that it was shaped, as he says it was, by his urge to generate situations that would reveal not only the action of "affronting" destiny but also the young woman who did the affronting. For Roland Barthes, Tzvetan Todorov, Algirdas Greimas, and Claude Bremond, the action in narratives is foregrounded and becomes the chief locus of interest. Even in working with narratives in which a considerable interest in characters might seem to be evident, these critics subordinate character to other elements in the narrative, and chiefly the narrative structure itself.

A curious verbal usage reflects the shift in focus and valuation that we have been examining. Both scholarly and popular discussion of narrative and drama had focused on the motivation of characters. Late nineteenth- and early-twentieth-century criticism took this for granted, as we can see in A. C. Bradley's analysis of the motives of Hamlet or Iago; in Leo Tolstoy's discussion of what he took to be the faulty motivation of *King Lear;* and in William Archer's panegyric on Ibsen's skill in revealing his protagonists' motivation.[26] Such critics assumed that characters exist and have motives for what they do. They took it as self-evident that we can reflect on such motives and learn who the characters are as well as what their author was telling us about them—and about the world. Formalist and structuralist discourse, however, applies the term *motivation* to the formal rationalization of narrative sequences—that is, the justification on pseudorational or formal grounds of what happens. It is no longer the people active in the story that are "motivated" in making things happen but rather the logic of the narrative itself. When that logic simulates the logic of possible events in the real world, it is designated "realistic motivation"; when it follows the conventions of an art form, it is called "artistic motivation."[27]

The structuralist prejudice against thinking of character in terms of psychological motivation is so strong that a broad spectrum of readers has come to think that earlier critics virtually invented the figures they encountered in narratives. Rejecting the older novelistic traditions of discourse, Barthes, in 1966 insisted that character must be subordinated to plot; that the notion that characters possess a "psychological essence" must be totally eschewed; and that we must view characters exclusively as participants in spheres of action. The latter notion was snappily summed up by Todorov (1967) when he held that the literary characters whose motivation (in the psychological sense) we may be tempted to analyze are in fact only the sequence of all the subjects of all the verbs in a story. Although Barthes later (1970) qualified this view of character and even formulated a separate "code" for dealing with character, the main trend of structuralist discourse has followed his earlier view.[28]

On the whole, the structuralists have held that character does not emerge as a detachable or independent element in our consciousness during or after reading. Nor is character to be thought of as part of that realm of existence that figures in the text itself. Rather, it is, in a manner of speaking, dissolved in the sequence of events and images in the text and cannot be fleshed out or imagined as possessing coherence in its own right.

Gérard Genette's essay on verisimilitude in literature (1969) reveals the scale of values implicit in the structuralist view. Genette holds that in narrative, "unmotivated" actions are superior to "motivated" ones; that is, he holds that "pure" narratives, which set out bare, unrationalized sequences of events, are to be valued more highly than narratives whose presentation strives to expose the logic of events.[29]

Todorov's "narrative men" (1967) are fit emblems of such a narratological notion of character. They are the kinds of characters that appear in nearly "pure" *récits* such as the stories of *The Arabian Nights*, where the qualities of the "agent" involved in the story are mentioned only because they are to be manifested in action at the earliest possible moment. For example, the reference of the trait "cowardly" is not to a character as "coward" but to the necessary action that is performed, which is "cowardly."[30]

More radical than the common garden-variety structuralists and structural narratologists are such semiologists as Greimas (1966) and Bremond (1973), who seek to assimilate character not to the logic of the narrative's surface structure but to the narrative's geometrically schematizable depths. For them characters figure as ciphers that perform the functions needed to realize a schematic paradigm of narrative elements that underlies the "surface" of the story. Since all stories are reduced, in such analyses, to patterns of possibility even tighter and more narrow than those of the folktale, it is not difficult to conceive of the characters as functioning in such a manner. In the semiologists' readings of narrative, as in Propp's, characters are divested of their named specificity (however great or limited to begin with) and reduced to *actants*—performers of transactions such as giving and taking, supporting or betraying—within the underlying scheme, which is formal and logical, not thematic.[31]

In effect, the semiological approach to narrative is an effort to formulate a "grammar of narrative" within which the issues are not thematic or in any way referentially related to the world of feeling, action, or thought. Rather, the issues are purely structural. Theorists seek to define the "syntax" of stories—that is, the way they are constructed of given paradigmatic elements that can be combined and recombined without reference to meaning.[32]

The most radical semiotic position goes further and moots the possibility of completely discarding the idea of characters as entities—even as agents, actors, or *actants* in a coded sequence of events. Here even the initial structuralist view that character is no more than the sum of all of the subjects of all of the verbs in a text is abandoned. Characters are dissolved within the linguistic texture of a work and do not add up at all—not even as the subjects of all the verbs.[33]

In both its more radical and its less radical versions, structuralism tends toward a thorough desubstantiation of character in literature even when structuralist critics discuss the issue of character. Thus, even when critics with affinities for this tradition have engaged the problem of character, they have tended to reject the possibility or desirability of dealing with it in itself. Both Leo Bersani and Hélène Cixous, for example, take the view that the notion of character is a repressive notion and that writers, in trying to represent character, merely reproduce the falsifying masks imposed by society—what Lawrence called "the old social and moral ego of the character." Bersani and Cixous assume that consciousness,

the will, the need to make choices, all of which are traditional elements of the self and have been central to the representation of people, are only fictions of a repressive society. The
"reality" of people is therefore elsewhere, either in their
instincts or in the clash between the instincts and the repressive
agencies of society, including the ego. To deal with the reality
of people is therefore to subvert the socialized self and to
depict (or, for the critic, to exhume) what underlies it. It is
therefore to define configurations of experience that do not
resemble people as traditionally conceptualized.[34]

When conceived as a figment within a fiction, character
becomes one of several dimensions of unreality—of a
constructed unreality that fills the world of literature. Indeed,
in the highly self-conscious and self-reflexive postmodernist
fiction, which shares its assumptions with post-structuralist
and deconstructionist views of "the text," we witness the
dismantling of characteristic modes of generating character.
Such dismantling takes place at the very moment we might
expect the characters who figure in the work to be generated.

Self-consciousness about how texts are generated—and its
accompanying self-reflexiveness—is of course, nothing new
in literature. Renaissance texts, for example, are full of it, as
in Shakespeare's highly self-conscious dramatic art, which
makes us see how the delusions of the lovers in *A Midsummer
Night's Dream* are generated and how Othello's green-eyed
monster comes into being. Similar underscorings of psychic
and literary process are to be found among the early texts in
the tradition of the novel, as in *Don Quixote*, where the
"literary theme" serves to underscore the fact that the Don,
who can't tell what is in a book from what isn't, is himself in
a book that is made up in part of other books, and comes to
be known in the world as a character who emerges from a
book. Or consider *Tristram Shandy*, where the deliberate
highlighting of the puppetlike simplicity (and monstrosity) of
My Father and Uncle Toby serves as the ground for genera-

ting their "characters," which come alive *through* their hobbyhorsicality.[35]

The difference between postmodernist and earlier literary practice in the generation of character is that even in the process of signifying and underscoring the artifice through which his characters are projected, a Shakespeare invites us to envision them as substantial hypothetical beings, possessed of whatever quiddity the text solicits us to bestow upon them. The same, in more limited ways, is true of *Don Quixote* and the figures in *Tristram Shandy*. We respond to the solicitation that we "add them up," that we compound them of the elements given us and relate to these emergent images as entities analogous to human beings whom we know in life.

Postmodernist fiction, on the other hand, not only asks us to reflect on the ways in which character is fabricated, in our consciousness as well as in literary texts, but also often frustrates our construction of character altogether. The "new novel" in France takes as axiomatic the refusal to generate characters in the old sense. Nabokov's *Real Life of Sebastian Knight* goes still further. It not only contemplates the process by which we fabricate the images we have of people in art as well as in life but stresses the necessary falsity of such images and their dissolution into absurdity, on the one hand, and into the text (or even into the fabricator of the text) on the other.[36]

The Real Life of Sebastian Knight was published in 1938, but it anticipates the entire postmodernist project with regard to character, as it does with regard to other aspects of fiction. Nabokov not only pits the fictions that animate and inform the "real" life of Sebastian Knight against the fictions that seek to evoke the "reality" of his life but also refuses to allow V.—its narrator—or "his" reader to form a coherent image of Sebastian. All of the images of Sebastian Knight, as they emerge from the novel's elaborate structure of fictions, assertively refuse to add up to a single image, not to speak of a single motivational system. In the end we have no coherent or comprehensible Sebastian Knight. Despite the elaborate comedy of mistaken identities in the novel, there is no single Sebastian Knight entity for us to embrace. It is impossible for the reader to take hold of Sebastian, except possibly as a consummate cliché, that of the mysterious and mystifyingly elusive Romantic artist.

The elusiveness of Sebastian Knight—the impossibility of forging the disjunctive manifestations of his "being" into a single, memorable image of a particular person—is part of Nabokov's high artifice. Here that artifice is committed to making us aware of the artificiality of character in both art and life and to neutralizing the substantiality of character as an element in the novel.

Such neutralization is part of the program of the post-modernist movement in criticism as well as fiction. Criticism and critical theory go further than fiction in that they extend such neutralization backward in history. It is not only that current fiction eschews people—in the way that current "reality" may forgo them—but that current criticism extends this rejection to the world of earlier literature. Nabokov merely denies us access to the hypothetical existence of Sebastian Knight; Barthes, Genette, and those who come after them deny even the hypothetical existence of Hamlet or Anna Karenina as intelligible beings or as coherent constructs that are imaginable in their own right. Jacques Derrida and his followers go further and come close to denying the existence even of people in life as anything but fictions constructed in our minds.

2

On the Reality of
Character in Literature

Recent theorists—structuralists and post-structuralists among them—have consolidated the case against character in literature. Having done so, they must face the question of what we are to do with characters who stand outside the canon of postmodernism. There is no doubt that their skepticism gives them a privileged view of certain texts—those of post-modernism, which they interpret as no one else can. They are no less advantaged with regard to the self-reflexive texts from the past that inspire their tradition.

In relation to very considerable portions of the literature that we inherit from the past, however, both the structuralists and the New Critics stand rather helpless. Unless we take the view that the critical consensus of virtually all preceding epochs of literature was based on a delusion, we must deal with the fact that the canonical texts of the Western literary tradition have seemed to readers to deal with people and to project powerful images of discrete human beings. Indeed, the characters who figure in the classical texts have elicited responses that are closely analogous to the responses people have had to other, real people, contemporary or historical. We need only look at the Alexandrian commentaries on Homer or at the rabbinic and patristic commentaries on the

Bible to see the extent to which human behavior, as reported in the sacred texts, was seen to invite interpretation and understanding on common-sense as well as theological grounds. Such grounds always involved questions of motivation and the assumption that the agents in any action had, or should have had, the coherence of identity and intention that we expect of people in real life.

The gods, to be sure, might seem to be an exception, not because they were not motivated but because of their wildly metamorphic propensities. However, their unpredictable transformations merely highlighted the fact that mortals were different, and that only under magical, demonic, or divine possession could they lose their human shape or the coherence of their ordinary selves. Character and ordinary human motivations were ignored, however, in allegorical readings of these texts, as in many Alexandrian readings of Homer or in Philo's readings of the Bible.

Still, there is no question but that readers in past times— ancient, medieval, and early modern—tended to understand texts in terms of character, among other things, and that when character was read, it was read in terms of motivation. No one speaks more eloquently to this assumption than Aristotle, even though he subordinates character to plot in tragedy. For Aristotle, character, when it figures in texts, is seen to function in terms of the ordinary laws of psychological causality: the laws of love, hate, jealousy, and other emotions.[1] Dante, too, despite the allegorical dimension of his work, assumes the "literal" or "historical" reality of his people and depicts them in terms of their given, assumed, or natural emotions. Their symbolic meanings within the allegory, at whatever level, are projected through figures whose feelings and motives are natural.[2]

Renaissance drama, as well as the novel throughout at least its first 150 years, was no less insistent on the reality and the actual or potential unity of characters it contained. Both literary criticism and literary traditions attest to this, and criticism still more articulately than the literature it engaged.

Thomas Rymer, in the seventeenth century, declares that *Othello* is a bad play because Othello is a bad man with bad motives.[3] Such emphasis on motives peaks in Maurice Morgann's eighteenth-century essay on Falstaff, which elaborately pursues the question of the kind of man Falstaff really is and how we are to judge him on the basis of that. Morgann is notorious among twentieth-century readers because of the lengths to which he goes to defend Falstaff's goodness and thus to justify our affection for him. Morgann's argument is grounded on the assumption that we can take an impression of Falstaff's real nature, which is *there*, behind all the falsifying appearances in which we are entangled as we watch his shenanigans.[4] Tolstoy, writing about Shakespeare, and William Archer, discussing the drama, employ similar assumptions about the quiddity of characters and the possibility of ferreting out both their natures and their motives.[5] So have discussions of the novel, throughout its history.[6]

Obviously, there are deep problems in psychologizing about Jacob's feelings when he found out that it was Leah he had married and not Rachel, or in construing Helen of Troy's character on the basis on the Homeric texts. The problems are no less great in trying to define the relationship between surface and depth in Falstaff or Hamlet or between contradictory aspects of surface behavior in Edgar or Edmund in *King Lear.* And the problems are compounded when, as with Homer, the Bible, and certain of Shakespeare's plays, scholars have not even been able to establish the unity of the texts themselves, and therefore have not been able to provide even minimal textual grounds from which to gather evidence as to the character of the characters.[7]

Yet whatever the problems of conceptualizing and interpreting character, literary characters *are* generated by the texts in which they subsist and participate in whatever reality literature itself generates and participates in, even in works that dismantle themselves before our very eyes. As critics have tried to show, with greater or lesser effectiveness, literature—

whether read as fiction, or heard as oral narrative, or viewed as drama and film—involves the generation in our minds of images of people who figure in it. Hence we must have a way of talking about such images, about their nature and function—doubly so, perhaps, because, to judge by the history of the critical tradition, we often respond to these images with an intensity and a degree of both affectivity and objectivity that are greater than what we feel for people we encounter in life.[8]

Any way we seek or find to talk about characters in literature must, to be sure, take into account the issues raised in the critique of character that has been conducted over the past fifty and more years. It must incorporate the consciousness of the hypothetical and constructed—the fabricated—nature of literature that has been at the heart of that critique. It must acknowledge the difficulty of retrieving any "original" meaning for a received text or context, ancient or modern. And it must strive to confer on characters in literature (and related modes of discourse) no more "reality" or verisimilitude than their texts legislate for them.

Along these lines, it seems to me that there are several basic things to be said, things that have been touched upon in recent discussion of the issue. One is that if character is to be dealt with at all as an element in its own right, it must be dealt with as an aspect of the surface structure of the text, as one of the relatively complex and relatively independent interlocking elements that constitute the text. There are other structures in a text, and levels of meaning other than the one at which character as a thing in itself subsists. But if we are to deal with character as such, we must begin with the level at which character exists. That may be said to be the first, most evident, utterly manifest level of the text, the level at which we appropriate the elements of the text from the verbal signs that constitute it. That is, character in literature, as we ordinarily think of it, is generated by the words that point to structured sequences of events within the work. Character can, of course, be generated by other means. On the margins of literature stand ritual, silent films, pantomimes, picture books, and the like, which generate images of people by nonverbal means. These means, however, are analogous in their modes of operation to verbal or strictly literary means, since they project their characters in terms of culturally sanctioned signs.

A second rudimentary but crucial point is that the means of generating images of characters do not in themselves *constitute* character; they *signify* it. Character in itself does not exist unless it is retrieved from the text by our consciousness, together with everything else in the text. But it can be retrieved, provisionally and for the sake of pleasure or understanding. Character is, as Rickword insists, separable from the text, along lines dictated by the text.[9] Characters do not "live" between the covers of a book; Constantine Levin and Othello are not homunculi contained in the works they figure in. They, like everything else in the text, exist meaningfully only insofar as they come to exist in our consciousness.

According to this view, our experience of character is the end product of a process implicit in reading, the *"final cause,"* as Rawdon Wilson puts it, of character in literature. Wilson, in the latest of his essays on character in literature, published in 1979, offers a handy scheme for defining available approaches to character. His scheme is organized along the lines of Aristotle's four causes: material, efficient, formal, and final. The material cause, as Wilson sees it, is the writer, in whose imagination characters take form. The efficient cause is the text, within which the characters are projected. The formal cause is the artifice that forms, generates, or precipitates character within the text, so that it is "there" in the text for us to appropriate. And the final cause is the impact on us of those figures, an impact that has deep moral and psychological roots and implications in human experience.[10]

Wilson himself comes to hold that it is the final cause—the impact element—that is ultimately what interests us in character. I agree with him wholeheartedly. In its very title, Wilson's essay reveals the paradox that is at the heart of his conception of character and, essentially, of my own. His essay is titled "The Bright Chimera: Character as a Literary Term," and it vividly establishes, by way of anecdote, that character is at once an extremely vivid entity—an entity as real to the imagination as the table in one's room—and a highly delusive one. Wilson insists that we experience characters in fiction as having the reality of people, and sometimes as having more than such reality—but also as not existing at all. Using an anecdotal approach, Wilson deals with the question of the referentiality of the discourse in which characters figure: the question of who and where characters are, and of what kind of reality they represent. In effect he grants all of the difficulties raised by the chimerical quality of characters, at the same time that he insists on their reality for us.

Although he does not specifically say as much, Wilson is responding to positivist questions concerning the reality of what literature is and what it refers to. He is also working along the lines of the early, conservative reader response theory, already formulated by Roman Ingarden by 1931 and developed by Wolfgang Iser in the 1970s—the theory that insists on the role of the reader in constructing (or retrieving) the literary work.[11] Reader response theory is concerned with how our sense of what is in a text is generated, both by the text and by our activity in appropriating or realizing it. The emphasis on our activity is crucial, because it reminds us that the whole which is the literary work is not only the sum of its parts, and more than the sum of its parts, but also a conjuring of absent, nonexistent parts. A work of literature is an entity made up of things not there, referred to by the words that constitute the text. Even the things "not there" —houses, people, events—are "there" only insofar as we fabricate them in consciousness out of what we bring to their perception: that is, out of our experience, and out of what we bring from our experience to the work we are reading.

Rawdon Wilson, to be sure, does not take up the theoretical issues involved in this view. He pays no heed to the process whereby the "bright chimeras" of literature—its characters—are retrieved from texts or projected into them. Nor does he ask why and how certain characters challenge us and our presuppositions so effectively. Among recent critics directly concerned with character as such, only Seymour Chatman (1978) and W. John Harvey (1965) have pondered the questions of retrieval and challenge with any effectiveness. And they have pondered them from very different, though compatible, grounds—grounds that seem useful in defining the nature and substance of character in literature.[12]

Seymour Chatman, who works within the terms of structuralist and post-structuralist poetics, insists that character is retrieved from texts as a cumulative image that is consciously or unconsciously extrapolated and then rationalized as a paradigm of traits belonging to the character. In Chatman's view, the structuralist argument that character is the sum of the subjects of all of the verbs in a narrative is true up to a point but is finally inaccurate. He holds that narrative is linear, existing in a temporal dimension, and consists of the sequence of words and of events conveyed by the words. But he also insists that narratives, in their temporality, generate in our consciousness a spatial world of what he calls "existents," consisting of such elements as scene, setting, and character, made up of images that accumulate in our consciousness. Chatman holds that such images not only are generated by the text but achieve a certain autonomy in our minds. He notes that the experience of reading often involves the retention of our image of a character, not only apart from events but also long after we have forgotten the events.[13]

In effect, Chatman holds that as we read a story or watch a film, we apprehend the qualities of a character that are revealed by his or her speech, gestures, actions, and thoughts as well as by the reliable or unreliable accounts that we get from the text itself, including what other characters say about that character.

These qualities, encoded in the impressions we take from

the text, result in an image of the character and then, if we make the effort, in a rationalized conceptualization of the character. The latter takes the form of a "paradigm of traits." Both image and conceptualization, in Chatman's account, detach themselves from the context of words and images in the text and take on an existence of their own. Hence the possibility of remembering Anna Karenina and Hamlet long after we have forgotten everything else about the texts that generate them—even, or especially, the language that brings them into being.[14]

Chatman is interesting and useful in his reasoning upon the process of our retrieval and construction of character. He is no less interesting in his insistence on the congruity between the process whereby we fabricate our conceptions of "real," historical people and the process whereby we construct images of characters in literature. Chatman makes the telling point that our knowledge of Samuel Johnson, who really existed and whose existence is heavily documented, is as much a construction of our minds from written evidence as our idea of Hamlet or Anna Karenina. In both cases, Chatman holds, we extrapolate the paradigm of traits that distinguishes the person, and in both cases we constitute such a paradigm in terms of what Chatman takes to be the only terms we have for talking about people at present— namely, trait-names. Referring to the work of Gardner Murphy, Chatman notes that trait-names are the repository for what we know and think about people, and that, whatever their limitations, trait-names suffice in their richness and variety for all that we may want to say about people. He holds that we now have no better vocabulary for such discourse.[15]

In effect, Chatman makes an elaborate case for the affinity between characters in literature and people in life, and for the similarity between the way we retrieve them, conceptualize them, and respond to them. He goes further in this direction, in fact, than I have so far indicated. Chatman holds that retrieval and imaginative reconstruction of character permit and even mandate speculation on the past, present, and future of each character. His grounds for doing so are the "openness," as he terms it, that is made possible by the extrapolation of a paradigm of traits for the character—a paradigm that exists in the spatial dimension that we abstract from the temporal sequence of the action.[16]

Chatman is extremely skillful in highlighting the process of abstracting characters from text and in his insistence on using natural language for talking about them. He is constrained in his discourse, however, by the strictures of his theoretical position, which is more bound than I would wish by the verbal surface of the text: hence his cleaving to the trait-names system. In effect, only the word, in his formulation, links literature and life. I wish to go further and hold that more than the verbal terms of reference are at work. What links characters in literature to people in life, as we fabricate them in our consciousness, is the integral unity of our conception of people and of how they operate. I, indeed, want to go further than Chatman by holding that there is a profound congruity between the ways in which we apprehend characters in literature, documented figures in history, and people of whom we have what we think of as direct knowledge in life. In my view, even the clues that we take in and use to construct an image of a person are virtually identical in literature and in life.

I advance this argument in the face of the traditional distinction between "literary means" and "mimetic means" of characterization that is forcefully summed up by Yosef Ewen in his compendious *Character in Narrative* (1980). Ewen argues that characters are presented both in ways that reflect modes of self-revelation in life (for example, speech, gesture, and dress) and in ways that are characteristic of literature, as in the use of names, settings, metaphor and metonymy, and structured analogues with regard to character traits and behavior.[17] The problem with this distinction is that Ewen's "literary" means are not in principle "literary," any more than language itself is intrinsically literary. Even names, which might seem to be the most artificial aspect of characters in literature, correlate with social practice, since nicknaming and satiric naming are an integral part of our relation to people: this familiar "literary" strategy is used as a life element.

Given names, in life, are no less significant. To use structuralist terms, in being given a name, one is alienated into the "symbolic order." One's name indicates a whole variety of things, from origins and ends, as conceived by the culture into which one is born, to place in class structure and ritual order. Cohen is not Israel, and Israel is not Califargno, and the latter is not Wen Sung. Even personal (as opposed to clan or family) names are saturated with meaning. Think of all the Jewish babies who were named Alexander in the year in which Alexander of Macedon conquered Palestine, or of the West Bank and Lebanese children called Moshe Dayan or Jihad (Holy War, Crusade—against Moshe Dayan and his cohorts), or of the little American girls called Marilyn after Marilyn Monroe. Clearly, in life, name givers symbolize wishes and facts in the names they choose; so do takers of names in cultures such as that of the American Indians, where people take names in the course of initiation or other rituals. Name giving is a kind of limited scenario writing; one could regard it as analogous to the scenarios that Greek gods, or Nemesis herself, wrote—scenarios that men had to struggle with, scenarios that kept audiences panting to know how (or whether) some decree of fate would work itself out.

No less than names, analogues, metaphors, metonymies— even stylization—all exist in life, and we operate in terms of them when we "read" people, interpreting them. Think, for example, of how often we apprehend a person to whom people tell their troubles as "a big shoulder," or call a mean bully "an awful prick," or think that someone is "not a whole person" but a "caricature of himself," or muse, as Prufrock does, "I am not Prince Hamlet nor was meant to be," or think of ourselves and of others as "Hamletizing."

Such usage, in my view, is not a matter of life imitating

art, as Oscar Wilde quips, but a reflection of the fact that the prevailing forms of consciousness, as well as the modes, verbal and otherwise, in which we formulate them, are the same in both life and art. Nor is the issue only that idea that, as Howard Felperin points out in his discussion of Shakespeare, art re-presents life,[18] but that literature re-presents life in language, which is the medium in which our sense of reality is largely if not wholly formulated, and which contains, implicitly or explicitly, the residue of all the materials out of which everything literary, including character, is fabricated, even as it filters everything out of which our consciousness of people in life is formed.

In this view, both life and literature invite us to process figures who reveal themselves (or are revealed) in a great variety of ways: the characters' "own" speech, gesture, actions, thoughts, dress, and surroundings; the company they keep and the objects and subjects they desire, abhor, and equivo-cate about; the images and associations they stir in our consciousness, including the epithets that we apply to them. Characters in literature may seem to be distinguished by the fact that they are presented to us in reported discourse, in the signifying modes of a speaker or speakers, whether the speaker is a narrator or a fellow character. Yet it seems to me that this too is congruous, in form at least, to the way in which we receive and process data about people in life. In life too we hear and think this and that about others and note (or fail to note) that what we have apprehended is reliable or unreliable, coherent or incoherent, consistent or inconsistent. And in life, as in literature, we must extricate the people we perceive (or think we perceive) from the web of language and the film of appearances in order to form a clear (or unclear) conception of them.

Such a view is in effect very close to the substance, if not to the form, of John Harvey's position in *Character and the Novel*. Harvey holds that the process of retrieving character from fiction involves acts of reconstruction on the part of readers (or spectators), and that such reconstruction draws on readers' own experiences not only of people and the language in which we talk about people but of themselves. Harvey asserts, moreover, that the reality of characters, as well as their moral significance, derives from (1) what they draw upon in us and (2) our very effort to synthesize character on the basis of our experience, without reference to the kind of experience involved.[19] In effect, Harvey holds that in retrieving characters from the texts in which they are embedded we do not passively respond to them or even appropriate them. Rather, we constitute them out of the substance of our own experience. In the "reading out" of character, we read *in* as well—that is, we read into the text and its characters the configuration of our own experience and our consciousness of it. By this Harvey does not mean to suggest that we arbitrarily project ourselves into the characters in literature. Rather, he means that we validate the patterns of experience suggested by a text for the characters within it by recognizing them in terms of analogous patterns in our own experience.[20]

Chatman's emphasis is on the common denominator between the way in which we perceive and name characteristics in life and the way in which we perceive and name them in literature. His emphasis is essentially on the external: how we apprehend objects. Harvey's emphasis is on the inner process that precedes the naming and the construction of our images of characters. Harvey insists that from a moral and psychological point of view, the vitally meaningful aspect of literature lies in our involvement in processes that characters undergo and in our capacity (perhaps our compulsion) to create a gestalt of their being out of memories of our own analogous experiences—including, I would add, our fantasies. Harvey notes that even the shallow images of people projected in soap operas and other serial presentations are meaningful, and may even become richly laden with meaning, because over a period of time we bring an amplitude of association and feeling to them—something that makes them real for us, and gives us the feeling that they are like ourselves.[21]

In effect, Harvey describes a process that (with differences, of course) closely resembles both what psychoanalysts undergo when they interpret the behavior of patients and what all us less self-consciously experience when we "interpret" each other. The psychoanalytic literature, in recent years, has explored the modes of empathy—of entering into another person's experience—and of identification with others that psychoanalysts experience as they try to conceive of what goes on in their patients. The difference between our spontaneous response to characters in literature and psychoanalysts' responses to their patients is considerable. When we respond to literary characters, we in part abandon ourselves to fantasy, letting our feelings govern the direction of response. When psychoanalysts deal with a patient, they utilize their capacity for empathy and association of feelings in order to construct an image that they can check, and check again, against the evidence provided by the patient's behavior and associations. Yet it seems to me that the difference between these two kinds of response is not great. If psychoanalysts have the obligation to return from an inner exploration of feelings to the patient as he or she is, readers have the option of returning to the text and of ascertaining whether what they felt was suggested about a character is "really" there in the text—that is, really suggested by the elements of the text.

Before they reach the stage where they return to the text and check up on anything, however, readers undergo a complex process that is analogous to the one that is undergone by both psychoanalysts and ordinary observers of human beings. My account of Chatman has already suggested the nature of the process, but because of Chatman's emphasis on what I take to be the final, most deliberate stage of the process—the naming of traits—it seems worthwhile to outline the process briefly as I understand it. To begin with, both in life and in literature we register data, relatively "raw" data, involving human behavior. Even at an early stage, such behavior falls into patterns, which we then check against further data as they are provided to us. The process of checking is generally subliminal; images form before we are fully aware that they have formed, and we often respond to those images well before we distinguish the elements of which they are composed.

The naming of traits and the deliberate organization of traits into meaningful patterns generally come later in the process; we tend to analyze after we perceive. No doubt, to be sure, different people ratiocinate at different stages, working more or less intuitively, more or less analytically, according to temperament. On the whole, however, it is only late in the process of perception that we fully conceptualize our sense of characters, or of people, and come to reflect on the dominance or recessiveness of certain traits or on the relationship between one pattern of traits and another. Even where there is no complication or contradiction, it is only after a work or an acquaintanceship is over that we can say with certainty that a character is this or that, simple or complex, wicked or virtuous. For most readers, moreover, the image of a character in literature is formed before we become conscious of the language that generates the character, although this sequence may vary, depending on both the susceptibilities of the reader and the degree to which language is foregrounded in the text itself. Both in literature and life, moreover, the result of such reflection is a certain reductiveness; we reduce characters, as we reduce plots (or sequences of events), to what we take to be their essential meaning or their animating principle.[22] And often, in literature as in life, we find that a sequence of events or a series of traits lends itself to various readings, depending on the conceptualizations we bring to each reading and the perspective in which we place the material we have read.

The degree of fidelity of reader to text in the apprehension of character varies widely with the reader. There is always, in reading as in life, the permanent option of loosing oneself from the present data and losing oneself in fantasy about the characters one harbors in one's head. Such disengagement and its mechanisms, meanings, and values may constitute a legitimate subject of study for psychologists and even for students of poetics.[23] But this mode of response clearly violates the traditional conception of responsible reading, a conception that has been challenged in the course of the recent growth of interest in the reader and his or her prerogatives but that seems indispensable, at least in this context.[24]

If we feel bound by the limiting guidelines of the literary text, however, we run into a set of issues that have hounded readers at least since the onset of realism as the dominant literary mode. I mean the question of the correlation (or the lack of correlation) between the manifestations of human being in life and its manifestations in literature, and the corollary question of how we conceive of human being, identity, and consciousness in both.

Harvey himself, for all the amplitude of his conception of the moral life and of its place in literature, builds his argument on a set of assumptions about life and literature that, in my view, obscures some vital issues. He holds that we have one way of relating to ourselves and another way of relating to others, and that literature serves to break down the barrier between the two. In effect, Harvey recapitulates a familiar polarity, writing that "we have intrinsic knowledge only of ourselves and of people in literature—and extrinsic knowledge of others."[25] The crux is that literature gives us intrinsic, immediate, knowledge of others, knowledge such as we have of ourselves, and this becomes, for Harvey as for many others in the humanist tradition, the source of literature's moral value.

The difficulty in this position, for the study of literature at least, lies in the implicit equation between our "intrinsic" sense of ourselves and that mode of inward, mimetic, or representational rendering of character that most of us would recognize as equivalent to "round" characters in literature, as categorized by E. M. Forster in *Aspects of the Novel*. Forster contrasts "round" figures, which are full of conflict, surprise, and the possibility of change or development, with "flat" typological figures, whose sparse, simplified, mechanical, and stereotyped quality obviates change, development, or meaningful inwardness.[26] For Harvey, such flat, non-"intrinsic" characters are a problem because he assumes that literature should give us fullness of perception, feeling, and understanding. What then to do with "flat" figures, which provide no such thing? Harvey proposes two standard solutions. The first is that flat characters tend to be secondary—supporting—figures, which flesh out the world of the protagonists, whose experience is "intrinsic." The characteristic grotesqueness and energization of such figures are then seen to highlight and to help interpret the protagonists within the elaborated literary structures that generate them.[27] Hence we need not see the secondary figures as resembling ourselves; all we need to do is relate to the more complex and more fully realized inwardness of the primary ones, who are like us.

This is all very well and good as part of an argument about the moral value of literature and about literature's function in confronting us with our humanity and that of others. But it does not go very far in elucidating the intrinsic nature, value, and standing of the secondary figures: the ones that we can, by using Forster's shorthand, sum up as flat, or at least as shallow or limited. The second answer, which is often offered in tandem with the first, does not go much further. It holds that the extrinsic or externally seen figures are analogous to the round ones except that we see them from the outside and have no direct, authoritative "intrinsic" view of them. Implicitly, such figures, if turned around and opened up, would be "round."

The trouble with this answer is that it merely repeats the difficulty at another level. It posits the round or lifelike character, with whom we can easily identify, as the norm for literary representation and as the criterion for relating characters to life. In doing so, it supports the notion that the lifelike or life-related is "round," and the unlifelike and hard to relate to ourselves is flat. The truth, however, is that we are mistaken if we think that we are "round"—that is, rich, inward, ambiguous, and developing—whereas others, in their mechanical, attenuated, compulsive limitedness, are "flat." Mary McCarthy assaults the accepted view and holds that as social creatures and as creatures of habit or compulsion we are in fact debilitatingly, galvanically, or comically flat, as flat as the flattest Dickensian characters in literature. Any adequate view of character in life must allow that we tend to see ourselves as unique and as incarnations of intrinsic value, of which we have "intrinsic" knowledge. Any adequate view of character in literature must allow for a far wider range of possibilities. John Bayley allows for some such process when he holds that the greatest characters in literature —the most brilliant creatures of Shakespeare or Tolstoy— synthesize inside and outside views of an individual to create a kind of stereoscopic effect that is ordinarily absent from life.[28]

I wish to affirm the full congruity between the way we perceive people in literature and the way we perceive them in life, with all the possibilities of disjunction and synthesis that are available in the one domain being possible in the other. It seems to me that the sharp dichotomy that we tend to posit between the richness and "roundness" of our subjectivity and the schematism and reductiveness of our perception of others is as fallacious (if also as convenient, at times) as the dichotomy between round characters and flat ones, or between tragic characters and comic ones. For it seems to me that we "read' ourselves much as we "read" others, and that, as a variety of thinkers as different as G. H. Mead and Jacques Lacan have held, our reading of ourselves—indeed, our very sense of ourselves—is mediated by others, even as our reading of others is mediated by ourselves.[29]

Indeed, the images of ourselves have an enormous range, analogous to the range of ways in which characters are represented in literature. There are the nightmarishly grotesque ways we envision ourselves in self-hating dreams, where we enact ourselves with the fantasticality of figures in Spenserian or Boschian allegory or Gothic novels; there are the self-mocking images we have of ourselves as characters in third-rate melodramas or fourth-rate farces, as when we suddenly hear ourselves ranting in the clichés of a jealous husband or an irate mother in a bad movie; there is the self-inflated sense we have of ourselves as heroic figures, like the heroes of tragedy, the Lears and the Othellos, whose sublimity (never bombast!) redeems them from the common curse; and then there are the self-submerged images of ourselves as supersentient creatures of sentiment, like those that Proust evokes in his saga of selfhood and art. This last comes close to the Bergsonian unselfconscious and boundless sense of self to which John Bayley alludes when he says that "character is what other people have, 'consciousness' is ourselves."[30] Indeed, in a later chapter I will propose that there is a scale of simplicity and complexity, of comprehensiveness and partiality, of schematism (or stylization) and representationalism, of openness and closedness in our perception of ourselves and of others in life. And that scale or spectrum is directly analogous to the scale on which we perceive characters in literature.

So close is the congruity between our ways of perceiving and conceptualizing people in the two domains that it seems worth taking a critical look at another assumption about the relation between them. I refer to the tendency to insist on the type origins, and ultimately the type essence, of people in literature, and on the radically individual nature of people in life. Northrop Frye, for example, very engagingly insists on the type nature of characters in literature, holding as he does that all characters in literature grow out of the stock types of their genres. In Frye's view, the prototypical characters of the genres may or may not be elaborated into the appearance of individuality.[31] Georg Lukács, for his part, holds that although characters in literature may be highly individualized, their individuality is generated by typical

contradictions in the world out of which a literary work
grows. Lukács holds that packed into the dynamic individualized characters of literature are the prototypical animating
contradictions of the writer's world.[32] A kind of validation
for Lukács' view is the fact that certain characters in literature,
even when possessed of the greatest individuality, may become the names of types, as when we say that we are
"Hamletizing" or that someone suffers from Bovaryism.

Yet our perception of people is typological, in life as well
as in literature, just as all of our perceptions are essentially
typological and categorical. We tend to perceive anyone (as
we perceive any*thing*) in terms of some system or classification and only then come to conceive of him or her, if the signs
point that way, in terms of his or her uniqueness or individuality.
This is so in our daily experience, even though we may often
be disposed, within our conventions of perception, authentically to think that every person we meet is a unique individual.

Thus, when we encounter a new human figure, we note,
for example, whether it is male or female, white or black,
threatening or friendly, normative in appearance or odd.
Only afterward do we zero in on whether the oddness of,
say, an elderly, bowed, black, bag-carrying woman is the
oddness of a Dilsey, liberated from the pages of *The Sound and
the Fury,* or the oddness of a bag lady about to camp on the
sidewalk of New York's West Ninety-sixth Street. And if it is
a bag lady, only afterward will we "decide" whether to focus
on her as a particular human being, with an imaginable
personal history, or as a specimen of one of the many things
she appears to be: black, female, middle-aged, homeless, or
disoriented.

In effect, what we have done in the latter case is think of
the bag lady, as of everyone else we perceive, not as an individual but as a type, as a being who is grasped as one of the
typological series. And this holds both in life and in literature,
even with characters who are presented as radically individual and highly individualized. Indeed, it is equally true in our
perception of those nearest and dearest to us, to the extent

that we see even spouse, child, and grandchild in terms of their typical role functions. And it holds true whatever the typology we are working with: political, moral, psychological, theological, sexual, or literary.[33]

The advantage of such a conception of how we perceive character is that it gives us further grounds for insisting, with Virginia Woolf, that literature's way of projecting character is analogous to the skills that serve us in life, and for agreeing with Harvey that our ways of retrieving character from literary texts rest on those same skills, augmented, of course, by our understanding of the nature of the literary text and its constituents.[34] It also allows us to say that whether we think of character as mimetic (representational) or "poetic" (made), we exercise the same powers in the same ways. From the vantage point of the perceiver of character, apart from the crucial heightening of the language or the other presenting media, the cues by which we apprehend and interpret character are the same in life and in literature. A character in a play cannot attack us as we sit in the audience of a theater. We perceive him as an attacker, however, by the same signs that mark his counterpart in life. Similarly, although a seductive character on the stage cannot actually seduce us, we know the signs of its seductiveness because we know how to read them in life.

Just as we recognize the typefying nature of all perception, so we should also insist on the potentially schematic nature of character, in life as well as in literature, and on the possibility of reading character in life in terms of such schematism. Although the imaginative scope of literature permits degrees of fantasticality—for example, the perfect mutual attunedness of the Sicilian Brothers, or the many-headedness of Cerberus—impossible in life, it is important to note that within the range of what nature permits, life generates grotesques closely analogous to what literature portrays and projects. Here, I think, the nightmarishly consciousness-expanding horrors of our century have affected our way of perceiving reality, and this change must be taken into account. Nineteenth-century writers often seemed able to believe in normative limits to grotesqueness; faith in such limits seems more difficult for us now.

John Romano's *Dickens and Reality* (1978) makes some telling points in this regard. Romano rightly insists, with the structuralists, that verisimilitude is a relative notion, shifting from age to age and from culture to culture. Bearing this in mind, he holds that there is no reason not to think of certain characters in literature who have been regarded as "unrealistic grotesques" as in fact fair representations of what particular people might be like. He holds that a Miss Havisham or a Jenny Wren is a possibility conceivable within any spectrum of human types.[35] I would add that one possible way of reading certain kinds of extremely stereotyped and mechanical characters is to see them as examples of extremely neurotic character formation or of arrested development;[36] another is to see them as schematic reductions of social, moral, or historical types. Still, to place them in relation to life we need not read them as representations of people who might exist; it should be enough to recognize them as images of people that we might generate in our fantasies or our dreams.

Indeed, we need not move as far as Romano does in the direction of making forthright correlations between people in life and bizarre characters in literature. The essential point here is that we identify characters in literature in terms of qualities and of constellations of qualities that we know from life. And the range of qualities and constellations in life is very considerable. In our experience in literature, there are occasions when the codes of a work indicate that we are not to apprehend a character in terms of our experience, as when a text makes it clear that a character is symbolic of something other than itself. Even in such instances, however, we are free to consider what it is in our experience that such a character might correspond to. The exercise may be futile in many cases, but it remains a possibility: a fixing of meanings in frames of reference other than those established by the surface structure of the work itself.

This is what we mean when we say that we may, if we choose, "liberate" characters from a text and from the sequence of words, actions, and judgments that generate and trammel them. We ordinarily do not choose to do so. When we do, we are likely to make fools of ourselves, as when we talk about Ceres in a Shakespearean masque in terms of her own maternal impulse or discuss the oedipal difficulties of the actor who speaks the speech Hamlet asks him to speak. Yet it is important and necessary to acknowledge the potential legitimacy of even such excesses; without these theoretical possibilities we cannot make important literary distinctions and judgments, as we do, for example, when we ask what it is in the rendering of Pip's experience that makes the final Biddy episode in *Great Expectations*, in which Pip finds Biddy married to Joe, seem false, and the closure of the novel therefore problematic, or why the experience of the narrator in *The Turn of the Screw* can be read in two ways.[37]

When we go as far as I suggest we can in wrenching character from context, we are extending very, very far the "natural" disposition to read character in literature as we read character in life. Naturally, whatever system we use for reading the one we use for reading the other. We do so intuitively, as Woolf believed. But even intuitive readings are informed by theories and conceptions of character. Hence a critic should have a coherent view of character, a view that can encompass all of the people and the images of people that we encounter, in literature as well as in life. This is especially important if we are to develop a viable theory of character in literature.

There is, to be sure, no reason to insist on any single view. Every age has generated its normative conceptions of the human being and its own paradigms for dealing with deviations from those images. Yet it seems to me reasonable to suggest that the changing formal psychologies and the schemes for talking about character in literature share the assumption that people are subject to conflict and therefore undergo processes of development, psychic and social. Even Chatman's notion of paradigms of traits implies process, at least to the extent that it implies, in the reader or spectator, a progressive decoding of character as the narrative or drama unfolds, and also allows for the possibility of development in character. Yet in using the term *paradigm*, which suggests a static pattern, Chatman minimizes the possibility of dealing with the kinds of conflict and process that inform the characters we meet in literature and that also animate the works in which they figure. Any adequate conception of character must include some conceptualization of the kinds of conflict that are experienced by people in life and by their analogues in literature.

To read *King Lear* is, Keats wrote, to burn through "the fierce dispute / Betwixt damnation and impassion'd clay."[38] The kind of reader's experience that Keats describes—an experience of conflict—is normative for our involvement with literature and with the creatures who inhabit it. *Lear* is an extreme case, because of the ferocity of the conflict that it contains and the extent to which we are given access to both the conflict within people and the conflict among them. In neither literature nor life are we often confronted with contention quite so fierce. But the formulation nonetheless seems apt, suggesting that in literature we are engaged in the dynamic life of the characters and that what makes them meaningful for us is the kinds of conflict they embody and experience and the way those conflicts are articulated in the work.

Not all characters in literature, to be sure, are presented in ways that provide us with grounds for experiencing conflict in and through them. There are, as we shall see, characters who obstruct involvement with conflict, who are presented simply as possessing this or that trait or representing this or that value. When this is the case, we must perceive them for what they are, even as we ponder the reasons, literary and structural, for the absence of conflict and speculate on what the conflict might be if there were more manifest signs of its existence. In the end, we tend to think of character—of people, to begin with—in terms of conflict, which may be moral, social, or psychological in nature.

It is curious how pervasively our traditions of thought and feeling root any understanding of the world and of people in a sense of conflict. From Plato and Aristotle or Moses and Jesus onward this has been the case, and Hegel's conception of the world as contention and struggle is only the culmination of the tradition. Sigmund Freud elaborates a comprehensive vision of character that is grounded in conflict, and is probably the best view we have. For Freud, every feature, trait, and configuration of traits in an individual is the product of conflict. To read character, whether in literature or in life, within the Freudian scheme is to perceive the play of conflict and the patterns of its resolution in the individual.[39] In reading character in either life or literature, one moves from level to level, from surface to depth, from consciously formulated awareness of conflict to deeply buried inarticulate kinds of conflict that exist at the nearly brute level of instinctual life. In moving from level to level, we absorb information that we can use to hypothesize the whole structure of a person's development, and by virtue of that hypothesis to speculate on his or her concrete life history.

If we take a Freudian view of the fluid, conflict-ridden underpinnings of human beings, we may quite legitimately speak of character in literature in the wholly "open" way that Chatman opts for, even to the extent of speculating, in ways more sophisticated than the Victorian investigation of the childhood of Shakespeare's heroines, on the unexpressed past of the phantoms that we call characters in literature. We can do so with especial vividness and cogency when the works in which characters figure concretize their experience in rich, suggestive, and revealing ways that invite us to scrutinize the characters on the basis of rendered experience. One significant variable among literary genres, and also among the particular works that fulfill and embody the potentials of the genres, is the suggestiveness and directness with which they reveal the unifying system of conflicts that animate their characters.

Even a radical Freudian approach to character, however, does not mandate unremitting speculation on the life and experience of characters. Nor is a Freudian perspective indispensable for a conflict-centered view of character and its dynamics, although it is probably the most suggestive framework to use. Even readers who reject the Freudian conception of character inevitably speak of character in terms of conflict. Rawdon Wilson, for example, asserts that the "roundness" of round characters is a result of the vivid presentation of the internal value conflicts that they experience.[40] That, it seems to me, is a perfectly reasonable notion, but it does not go far enough in probing character as such. Its limitation is partly the high degree of consciousness with which values, as we ordinarily conceive of them, tend to be exposed and partly the extent to which value conflicts belong to the thematic structure of the works in which characters figure, with all the problems of reductionism that radical thematizations of character necessarily involve. [41] At the same time, if we read characters, like people, as fields on which values enact themselves in both conscious and unconscious ways, we easily convert "values" into categories such as "motives' and "impulses" and consider ways in which values are embedded in the deeper structures of motivation as well as the most manifest level of behavior.

Conflict, of course, need not be articulate or conscious, either for characters in literature or for people in life. Even the most articulate and conscious of characters—Lear, Hamlet, Rupert Birkin, Proust's Marcel—are driven by needs and conflicts of which they are not conscious. Paradoxically, the incandescent consciousness of such characters would seem to be rooted in the volcanic depths of whatever it is that animates them at the unconscious level of their being. It is just the levels of experience of which they are not conscious, and cannot be conscious, that fuel their frenzied discourse. Analogously, in even the most outrageously mechanical, unconscious, and inarticulate characters we find that it is conflict that renders them mechanical: as with Morose in *The Silent Woman*, or with Dickens's grotesques, or even with Melville's Ahab, who is consistently portrayed in terms of compulsive and mechanical energies. Indeed, Dickens, in his comic reductionism and his tendency to depict mechanical grotesques, is among the most relentlessly psychological of novelists, indicating the patterns of his characters' inner needs in the very fixity of their behavior and appearance.[42] The given terms of discourse in any text may not be identical to or even congruous with the terms of modern, not to speak of Freudian, psychology. But in the end they translate readily into psychological terms—that is, into terms that interpret behavior as a matter of impulses and motives—as do the traits that Chatman speaks of, or even the values in terms of which Rawdon Wilson analyzes Aziz in *A Passage to India*. Whether we are moralists or mystics or believers in behaviorist learning theory we tend to conceive of people in essentially psychological terms, and the task of inferring character (again, in literature as in life) from behavior is a psychological-interpretive labor that we perform instinctively and without reflection, all the time.

Even a conflict-centered psychological conception of character must, of course, go beyond an exclusively intrapsychic view of conflict. Lukács' Hegelian-Marxist notion of the individual and his traits as an epitome of characteristic contradictions in society is relevant here. This notion may play little direct part in our immediate apprehension of character, but it is indispensable in formulating our idea of the characters' animating conflicts, since personal conflicts ordinarily echo conflicts in the world, as Lukács holds. Indeed, given the centrality of such issues, Fredric Jameson's attempt to read literature in a Marxist way by cleaving to the structuralist and post-structuralist conception of character as function seems to me a regression from Lukács' view. Lukács' strength lies in the fact that, as I noted earlier in this chapter, he sees characters in literature as "themselves," but as selves that we can conceptualize in terms of the social and environmental conflicts that are played out through the characters.[43]

It seems to me that definition of a dynamic, essentially psychological model for talking about character provides a way of dealing with Barthes's objection to conceiving of character in terms of "psychological essence" and Richard A. Lanham's still more extreme identification of the traditional notions of character with Platonic essence, or soul.[44] In principle, even traditional conceptions of people as possessing a single unitary identity do not predicate any such static view as Lanham attributes to them. The classical—Greek and Roman—conception of human character as a given—a "nature," as it were, to be realized—did not preclude conflict within the struggle to actualize a person's nature. Indeed, the Aristotelian model mandated conflict; for Aristotle, a man's character is not given, but achieved through struggle.[45] And the Romantic and post-Romantic notion of struggle and development specifically necessitates the working through of potentialities within the self in the historical world. The Freudian model, which develops out of the Romantic model, still more dramatically posits not a static psychological essence but a set of dynamic psychological elements in ceaseless dynamic interplay. This interplay is so dynamic as to permit a thorough reinterpretation of earlier notions of self and soul, and therefore of earlier literary characterization. We may not be able to resolve conflict in fiction into its most radical unconscious components, as we are often able to do in life, but we can define those conflicts in terms of the same concepts that we use in life.

Such an approach makes it possible to deal with one of the more vexed historical issues in the reading of character, the question of how far it is legitimate to bring anachronistic notions of character to bear on texts, and how to bring them to bear. In answering this question, we must first acknowledge the fact that we retrieve figures from older literatures in terms of our own perception of character and of our perception of motives operative within character. We do so in regard to characters in literature exactly as we do in regard to historical figures. We must, to be sure, know what the author or compiler of the fable, saga, mystery play, or chronicle meant by the terms he or she employed, even as we must know (so far as is possible) the meaning of all of the words in the text and the significance of gestures and actions in the represented world of the texts. Thus a story of abduction and rape from a culture in which abduction and rape are part of a culturally sanctioned form of courtship would have a different meaning from a medieval Christian story that centers on the same elements. Similarly, we just know that when Chaucer tells us that his Prioress is "nice," he means something different from what we mean when we say someone is "nice."

One must, moreover, acknowledge the otherness of other epochs' conceptions of what a person is and of how a character in literature reflects that conception or responds to it. Clearly, different epochs conceive of people as well as actions in different ways, and so do different cultures. A comprehensive grasp of such variations would be useful not only for the study of people and societies but for the study of all of the artifacts—including the literary artifacts—that interest us.[46] So would a systematic analysis of the narrative patterns through which such conceptions are projected, patterns as necessary to our understanding of character as the language in which they are embedded.

Yet our retrieval of character from other epochs, from other cultures, and even from works that were the products of sensibilities different from our own rests upon a construction of the elements in the work on the model of the notions and responses available to us. We may allow for the fact that Othello, as Stephen Greenblatt argues, "executes" Desdemona because he believes that her unbridled love for him is "adulterous," in a meaning of the term defined by Renaissance divines. In the end, however, the salient fact about Othello is his murderous jealousy, whether the jealousy is based on a revulsion against his own sexuality or on a socially sanctioned judgment of Desdemona's. And we must factor that jealousy in terms comprehensible to us, even when we are intent on understanding and explicating it in historically grounded terms. To do otherwise is, it seems to me, to forgo the possibility of experiencing the things that Othello might mean to us—that is, to lose Othello as a viable object of response.

Hence, I am arguing, we have no alternative but to construct our images of character in terms of our own knowledge and experience. Even so extreme a view as Bruno Snell's about Homer's conception of the human individual—that Homer entirely lacked any such conception—cannot obviate our constructing Achilles or Odysseus in terms of our own conception of person, motive, and action. Such character construction, to be sure, is guided by the signs that we take from the text about the traits that belong to each character, about the scale on which we should engage with its inwardness, and about the range of issues seen to be relevant to its being. But the image that we derive is not wholly governed or determined by those signs. As long as we have clear signification of traits and of patterns of behavior, we are free to read them in terms of the gestalt we as readers get for the character.

To take a dramatic example, there is no reason not to link Achilles' crybaby behavior, when in his grief and humiliation he asks his mother, the goddess Thetis, for aid, to the heroic virtues—the aretē—that make him a hero. Similarly, we may relate the relative weakness that makes Hector Achilles' victim on the battlefield to Hector's stiff-necked resistance when Hecuba, his mother, bares her breasts and beseeches, by the dugs that suckled him, that he refrain from risking the safety of family and city for the sake of a fatal duel with Achilles. Indeed, Achilles and Hector may be seen as a matched pair of heroic figures, posed in postures of contrast with regard to the link between their male prowess and their relationships to their mothers. Homer surely did not "mean" us to read his characters in such terms. Yet there is no reason for us not to assume that he possessed such insights as are reflected in my reading, even if he had no conception of a unifying principle, or "soul," not to speak of a comprehensive psychology, for his characters. Nor is there any reason to assume that he would not accept such a reading if it were presented to him, although it is deliberately couched here in terms that are alien to the hieratic dignity of Homer's style.

Although it is true, as most scholars would affirm, that the modern conception of character arose sometime in the eighteenth century, more or less simultaneously with the rise of the novel, the patterns of behavior projected in earlier texts, all the way back to Homer and the Bible, lend themselves to interpretation along lines congenial to us—lines often shaped within the novelistic mold. The possibility—indeed, the necessity—of such reading seems to me so vital that the only limit I can see to its application arises when writers—usually postmodernist writers—deliberately try to prevent it. Such efforts, which have antecedents in earlier texts, are marked either by refusal to signify traits with any clarity or by the provision of a trail of red herrings to prevent the emergence of a meaningful pattern of traits. Nabokov, with his systematic mockery of Freud and also of realism in the representation of character, comes to mind again as a case in point. His anti-Freudian Freudian "clues" are meant to head off "interpretations" of behavior.[47] Yet even in Nabokov, it seems to me, the obstruction of coherence of character cannot wholly obviate our construction of coherent images of character. Beyond Nabokov, of course, are a variety of writers who strive for more or less "zero-degree" characters—that is, for the utter absence of characters as significant components of their fictional worlds. Yet even here—say, in the *nouveau roman*—it seems to me that obstruction of image formation or refusal of coherence and concreteness cannot prevent us from constructing possible, if possibly bizarre, images for interpretation, as in my facetious reading of Sebastian Knight as elusive Romantic artist.

What such readings of any particular text are worth depends on a variety of things, including the subtlety, interest, and complexity of the character presented, the nature of the issues for which the character is a vehicle, and the centrality of the character to the work itself. Clearly, unless we are interested in creating a "gallery of characters" from literature just for the sake of having one, there is no point in the random isolation and exploration of characters from texts in terms of whatever psychological or moral system we use. Yet the possibility of abstracting or "liberating" the characters and contemplating them as they are in themselves must be affirmed, for the sake of a full envisionment of the scope of individual texts and of the imaginative scope of literature itself. After all, characters do exist in literature, and unless we want to reduce them to minimal functions or archaeological curiosities, we must have some way of talking about them. Acknowledging life as the source of the whole spectrum of characters in literature and granting that we perceive people on models analogous to them, even though we distinguish sharply between them, seems as good a way as any, and a better way than most.

3

Homo Fictus, Homo Sapiens

In effect, our retrieval, or reading out, of character is guided by our consciousness of what people are and how people work. To read character adequately we must heighten our consciousness of the reciprocity between character in literature and people in life—between Homo Fictus and Homo Sapiens. We must be aware of the close kinship between the images we form in our minds of the one and the other, but also of the difference between the originals. To deal with people in literature, we must remember that they are not alive, even as we must bear in mind that people in life must not be treated like characters in literature. For Homo Fictus and Homo Sapiens are far from identical. To deal adequately with either, we must distinguish between them, both in themselves and as they take form in our minds.

To begin with, the imaginary beings who get into literature and who come swarming out of it into our consciousness are not people. They do not exist, except in our imaginations or as words on a page. They do not breathe; they have no body warmth; they cannot assault or embrace us. Nor do they figure as objects of our activity, except of our responsiveness. We cannot reason with them or interfere in their lives, any more than we can interfere with the lives of the dead. I may want to stop my brother from murdering his wife, and I can try to stop him, possibly even to some effect.

I can do no such thing when Othello is about to strangle Desdemona; all I can do, if I am watching the play, is bother the actor who is playing Othello and interfere with the pleasure of the audience in the theater.

Indeed, if the characters in literature are like people at all, in the ordinary sense, they are like dead people. The characters in literature, once they are "written," are finished like the dead. We can manipulate them only to the extent that we respond to the signs that generate them in our imaginations and, beyond this, only to the extent that we "liberate" them utterly from the texts that generate them and allow them to inhabit our thoughts, our fantasies, and our dreams. In fantasy we can make love to Anna Karenina as much as we can to Marilyn Monroe or the girl next door, and we can dream that the mad Herakles, wielding his club, is our father, just as we can dream that we are descended from Attila the Hun or that our own mother is enthroned as the Queen of the Damned in Hades or as Alice's Queen of Hearts. When we do so, however, we are violating their nature as characters in literature, who derive their legitimacy from the context that generates them—the text that provides them their local habitation, even their name.

Characters in literature, moreover, often lack even the appearance of unity that people in life ordinarily have. Characters cannot, of course, have real life histories, and they need not have imagined ones either.[1] And they need not be unified. This is not so with people. Within the central philosophic and psychological tradition of the West, we tend to assume that people in life have such histories and that they evolve within them as unified, and possibly unique, beings. We assume, in short, that everyone is possessed of an organically developed unity of being. We tend to make this assumption despite all the necessary complications of any simple notion of literal identity: despite Hume's challenge to the concept of personal identity, and despite the theoretical issues raised by the facts of individual development, amnesia, and schizophrenia.[2] The fact that we live inside our own consciousness and experience ourselves in the irreversible flow of time makes it impossible for us to prove we are the single thing we might wish to affirm we are. And the clinical facts of split personality or loss of consciousness of self calls into question any simple affirmation of unity in the self. Yet in life we do assume that apparent discrepancies, discontinuities, and contradictions in individual behavior and consciousness can be resolved by exploring the total life history of the individual. Such exploration, we tend to think, will reveal the roots of apparent changes or contradictions in character.

In life, moreover, there is a potentially endless amount of information that we can gather about a person. This, quite obviously, is not true of even the most richly elaborated characters in literature. If anything, what must strike us about characters in literature, as compared with people in life, is the relative meagerness of information about them and (the other side of the same coin) that this information tends to be very highly organized. Such organization opens the way for clearer, more stable, and more authoritative elucidations of behavior and personality than those we ordinarily achieve in life. The structure of narrative, on which elucidation of character largely rests, is *given* in literature, once a text is written. It must be constructed in life, if the shape of a person's life—the pattern of his or her character—is to emerge.

Here we touch one of the central paradoxes in the relationship between people in life and characters in literature. We postulate the unity, coherence, and complexity of people in life, and we tend to acknowledge the existence of a plethora of information about them that might open the way to understanding of the ground of that unity. In practice, however, one of the maddening aspects of our experience with people is the difficulty of getting at relevant information and the way in which the information, once we have it, resists definitive interpretation within any single system, within any meaningful story line. Ironically, literature, despite the relative meagerness of the information it provides, has the potential for projecting coherent and meaningful images of people—of "people" who are not people at all, but only characters in literary texts.[3] The very fact that they are characters in texts gives them their peculiar vividness as images of possible people and challenges us to respond to them and to interpret them by analogy to the way we interpret people in life. Because they are not real, we imagine them by analogy to real people and feel we know them better than we know real people.

This paradox is the basis for some of the curious things that have been said about character in fiction. E. M. Forster, for example, holds that the crucial difference between Homo Fictus and Homo Sapiens lies in the incompleteness of our knowledge of people in life and our impression that we know the people in literature wholly and exhaustively. Forster writes that "we can know more about [Homo Fictus] than we can about our fellow creatures." Elsewhere he says that "Moll Flanders, Amelia and Emma cannot be here . . . because they are people whose secret lives are visible. . . . We are people whose secret lives are invisible."[4]

Forster's formulation obviously is offered in "a manner of speaking." He is not saying that we know everything about the characters in a novel, but that we know everything we *need* to know about the characters, and that all such knowledge is meaningful. Forster's point is closely akin to a point that Rawdon Wilson makes about the quality of the knowledge we have about characters. Wilson stresses the obscurity and unreliability of the information we can have about living people, and its lack of cogency. In this context, he cites a well-known passage from Proust's *Remembrance of Things Past* where Marcel speaks of reveling in the novelist's happy discovery that fiction can enchant readers by opening for them a window into the opacity of the human heart.[5] "Actual persons," Wilson writes, "are invariably, in Proust's expression, 'opaque.' If they possess motives, those motives elude one. . . . Characters, on the other hand, do seem to have motives and values—or at least they often do, which is vastly different from the case of actual persons, who, I suspect, *never* do, in any clear sense."[6]

I would take issue with Wilson's insistence that we cannot read motives in life. But what is worth noting at this point is not the wrongness but the incompleteness of his view, as of Forster's. We know much more about people in life and could certainly know far more than we generally do. But our knowledge rarely has the definitiveness that fiction sometimes affords. The difference is not, as Forster might imply, that life is chaotic and opaque and art orderly and transparent but that our consciousness of life—that is, of people in life—easily lapses into incoherence, if not into chaos.

One reason for this is that most of us are not so skilled in reading human behavior as the novelists we admire. And we surely are not so skilled in registering and recording our sense of such behavior, even in our own consciousnesses. In life, moreover, we tend to be submerged not only in data but in experience as well—experience of ourselves, of others, and of the world. Most of us, even when we can gather and process the requisite data about others and arrive at a crystallized and clear consciousness of them, do not do so for long enough to form coherent and stable images of them or coherent accounts of their lives. Literature, like psychology and history, can stabilize and articulate such images and sustain consciousness of them. It can also make such images enduringly memorable because of the way it crystallizes them, facets them, and embeds them in words.

Such stabilized images differ from the images we ordinarily have of people in life. The organization of characters in literature rests on a stable, meaningful context of events and words that contain them. Wilson, working within the terms of his own conception, writes that "all characters are essentially schematic." One consequence of this radical schematism is that, as Wilson points out, "[the characters'] meaning cannot lie...in quantity of detail." Literary characters, he says, "provide less evidence than persons [in life], but it is a range of evidence that is inevitably more significant because it is not random, not cluttered, not mind-bogglingly vast." What confers meaning on character in literature is "the principle of organization behind the unrandom, uncluttered details of characterization."[7]

The organization, or schematism, does not reside within the characters alone. It is not just a matter of what is given within the self-contained limits of the characters—that is, it is not just a matter of the patterning of their responses, commitments, traits, and other features. If this were the case, the schematism of characters in literature would be no greater than the schematism with which we perceive people in life. In life, we perceive people in terms of wholly systematic patterns of perception and analysis—moral, psychological, political, or sociological—that help us to conceptualize them. The schematic organization of our knowledge of characters in literature differs from that of our knowledge of people in life in that the existence of characters in literature (and our perception of their existence) rests on the more or less coherent, more or less self-declaring structure of the work that generates them and that we perceive as a single thing. Even when we retrieve characters as relatively autonomous entities, we perceive them as part of an organizing structure made up of elements that are interfused with each other and that illuminate each other.

This structure exists at a variety of levels—verbal, narrative, motivational—and it lends itself to analysis in a variety of ways. The most productive, to my mind, conceives of the literary text as embodying a more or less highly structured and stabilized fantasy that, like a dream in the Freudian conception, organizes itself out of an underlying conflict and articulates itself in all the elements of the work. The characters themselves figure more centrally or less centrally in various works, but they always derive their qualities from the text as a whole. Indeed, when characters take shape in our imaginations as whole, coherent, consecutive creatures that seem analogous to the people that we know in life, the impression of their wholeness tends to rest not on them as they are in and for themselves but on them as they are generated and sustained by the text as a whole.

Characters, even when seen independently, must also be seen as part of the structure that generates them and contains them. This structure and its high degree of organization provide us with clues to the characters' personalities and motives that may be analogous to those we get in life but may also be more trenchant and coherent. Thus, although we bring to the interpretation of characters in literature the skills we use in "reading" characters in life, the patterns of meaningful evidence are somewhat different and tend to possess, as Martin Price and Wilson insist, a degree of coherence ordinarily absent in life. This schematism is coded into the entire structure of the literary work, giving us clues not only to the interpretation of character but also to the ways in which we are to "take" and "read" the characters—to the kinds of characters they are and to what we are to expect of them.

Because characters subsist within a complicated, stable phantasmagoria, within a given literary work each character tends to enter into mutually stabilizing and mutually illuminating relationships with all of the other characters in the work and with the elements that both generate and illuminate the characters. Examples are easy to find. As Janet Adelman brilliantly shows (1978), the familiar problems involved in interpreting the characterization of Edgar in *King Lear* can be resolved in this way. Edgar's character is, on the face of it, more than somewhat discontinuous as we see him in his triple role of ineffectual legitimate son, turbulent bedlamite, and vigorous avenger, who then becomes a potential restorer of order. The seeming incoherence (or multiplicity) of his identity has been read as a function of his instrumentality in making things work out as they need to and of providing still another voice in the chorus of madness in the play. Janet Adelman, however, shows that Edgar's triplicity can be resolved if we read him in the context of the seething anger that animates Lear himself and that pervades the play as a whole.[8] Similarly, the pattern of images of separation and fusion in *Wuthering Heights*, working together with the pattern of symmetry and contrast among different generations, illuminates and stabilizes our sense of Heathcliff and Catherine. And in *Middlemarch* and *The Portrait of a Lady* we learn something crucial about Dorothea Brooke and Isabel Archer (as well as about George Eliot and Henry James) from parallel images of jail and jailor, dungeon and dungeon keeper, which figure in the novels these characters inhabit, but which serve, because of difference in formulation, placement, and function, to communicate very different things.

Such figuration and configuration reflect the fact that characters in literature, as opposed to people in life, intrinsically mean something. They are part of a configuration of meaning that the work as a whole articulates, however obscurely. Such meanings, like everything else that matters in a text, exist at many levels, from the underlying, organizing fantasy from which the whole work springs to the thematic articulation in which the deliberate moral meanings of the work are organized. The last are usually the most obvious meanings in a text, and they are often at odds with the independent felt life of characters within it. The warping of characters to point a moral or adorn a tale is one of the more interesting problems in literature, and I shall return to it later in this chapter.

Yet even the thematic level, as a part of the whole configuration of a text, is vital for the study of character.[9] For characters are rendered palpable not only by what we know of them in themselves and from their interactions with others but also by the play of analogous structures, such as parallel characters and parallel situations, in both the action and the allusive texture of the work. Lear himself is fleshed out for us as a particular human being partly because another father (Gloucester) and his children appear in the play. The pattern of anger as a component of family situations that is refracted through Edgar and his analogues works in a different way. This pattern cuts across and under the manifest structure of themes in *King Lear*. It must be extrapolated on the basis of configurations of motive that underlie the manifest patterns and that surely underlie Edgar's conscious motivations. The pattern of parent–child relations, on the other hand, needs no such extrapolation: it is *there* on the thematic surface, manifestly there in the same way as the heath or the various residences in which Lear and his daughters live are there. And as a part of the obvious thematic structure, the pattern of parent–child relations creates a field for the self-manifestation of Lear and for the susceptibilities within ourselves out of which we construct our sense of him, as well as our response to him.

Pride and Prejudice still more conveniently illustrates the process by which a character is generated within a carefully woven pattern of meanings that sustain it and create the illusion of perhaps greater substance than is implied by the specific components of the character's rendered experience. Elizabeth Bennet is generated in a great variety of ways. One of them is the large number of directly rendered people and situations that we observe her responding to. Another is the way she is seen to react from within her own consciousness as she stands at the center of an action of recognition—that is, of confrontation with the elements of her own rendered experience. A third is the way the theme of first impressions of people is stated and restated within the experience of a great number of characters. That theme is reinforced by the dramatized issues of the marriage market and the stakes for which people play within it. But it reverberates within a set of analogous actions and situations in which people exemplify the frailties and foibles that threaten to make Elizabeth unhappy. Each of those people is faced with problems analogous to Elizabeth's; each is faceted in relation to those problems less complexly than Elizabeth, but complexly enough nonetheless. In the end, the pattern of parallels and contrasts in situation, in response, and in validity of response generates a field of meaning within which Elizabeth's quiddity and richness are in part generated. She belongs to a world that demands complex perceptions and responses of the reader, and she is also part of a pattern within that world, a pattern that centers on and articulates a theme for which her consciousness is a vehicle but of which her consciousness is also the product.

Pride and Prejudice, with its elaborate evocation of a protagonist who is complex, coherent, dynamic, and whole, illustrates another aspect of the function of the total context of a work in generating character. That aspect has to do not with the manifest structures of substantive meanings into which the character is cemented but with the more purely formal structure. I mean the way the organization of the whole text creates a space—an area where converging perspectives meet—within which the character subsists. Characters who stand at the center of a work, as Elizabeth stands at the center of *Pride and Prejudice*, are ordinarily flanked by lesser characters, of lesser complexity, dynamism, and wholeness. Such flanking characters usually serve compositional as well as thematic purposes, as with Jane Bennet, Charlotte Lucas, the rest of the Bennet sisters, Mrs. Bennet, Mrs. Gardiner, Georgiana Darcy, Lady Catherine de Bourgh and her daughter, down through Bingley's repulsive sisters and the housekeeper at Pemberley. The progressive diminution of centrality, repleteness, complexity, and interest creates the space within which the central character can be experienced in all her vividness, complexity, and coherence.[10] This "space" is analogous to the thematic dimension within which I have noted that Lear finds lebensraum, with the difference that here the space is generated by the formal disposition of the figures around Elizabeth. Clearly the same formal principle is operative in *Lear* as well, and in ways that diverge from the ways of creating the thematic and psychological space that I have touched upon.

It is not only the central figures of such large and substantial works as *Pride and Prejudice* and *King Lear* that convey a sense of *thereness* greater than the sheer bulk of what we know about them might seem likely to generate. Character, taking shape as it does in a field of stabilized dynamic fantasy and sustaining itself as an evidently coherent entity within it, may convey an impression of substantiality and complexity—often of sustained existence—even in the course of the briefest and most limited appearances. The idea, popular within nineteenth-century bardolatry, that every servant and every walk-on character in Shakespeare was designed to suggest implicitly individuated existence is obviously mistaken. But the possibility of the surprising animation, intensity, and fullness of figures that are very limited in the scope of their presentation remains. The heightened presence of such figures stems at least in part from the vivifying context of the work as a whole and of the thoughts, feelings, and fantasies that are pulled into the vortex of our responsiveness to it. Martin Price makes this point in an essay titled "The Irrelevant Detail and the Emergence of Form," where he speaks of how qualities and quiddities are generated within the field of dramatized interaction among characters and within the entire structure of themes and values that a literary work explores.[11] William Gass, too, even when holding that characters are no more than "words on the page," insists that the embodied details of a character's existence are the ground for configurations of identity that engage and challenge us deeply.[12]

The memorability of certain characters in literature may be attributed to the fusing power of the materials that coalesce within the stabilizing framework of the whole. The teleology—the purposiveness—of meaning, sustained by the underlying psycho-logic of the fantasy embodied in the work, charges characters with a vividness and intensity that rarely inform the personalities that we deal with in life.[13] The exception in life is encountered when we are in love with, or in hate with, someone and apprehend this person within a field charged with meaning by our internal needs. But in life the figures that we relate to are not stabilized for us, and they cannot be "played back" again and again as characters in literature can.

Literature, in short, has the capacity to charge relatively limited quantities of information with a sense of significance and to consolidate them into patterns of meaning. In the realm of character, this capacity leads to the heightening of something we know only too well from life—namely, the impulse to make constructs on the basis of limited information; to infer wholes from parts; and to generalize from those parts to the nature of the whole that they represent. In art as in life, glimpses of behavior—brief vignettes—are taken to be touchstones of larger being. In literature, the sense that we have "taken" someone's essence is often justified by the interpretive grace notes that a text ordinarily contains, grace notes that have to do with the high degree of organization in the text, with its compactness and its inner dynamism and elaboration. Chaucer, in presenting his pilgrims, is a master of such vignettes. Having read *The Canterbury Tales*, we feel that we have taken the essence—by which I mean, of course, the dynamic substance—of such characters as the Wife of Bath, the Prioress, and the Pardoner. In each case the patterning of surface detail, of implicit motivation, and of literary mode intensifies our sense of the *moto spirituale* (movement of spirit)—to use a term that Francis Fergusson borrowed from Dante—and the *moto psicologico* (psychological motion, or development from one point to another) that informs it.[14] In *The Canterbury Tales*, the framing of the various types of tales, with the different fictional levels and modes (realistic, fanciful, highly conventionalized, and fantastic) within the pilgrimage story, heightens, by modulated contrasts, our sense of the reality trapped within it. The substantiality of the pilgrims is set off by the variable fantasticality of elements in the tales in the way that the figures and scenes in the foreground of early Flemish paintings are set off by the stylized landscapes glimpsed in the background.

Language itself is no mean element in shaping, stabilizing, intensifying, and generalizing not only the characters in literature but also the fantasy in which they subsist. Language is at once the facilitating condition of literature—its medium—and one of its ultimate achievements. Poetry is not only "language highly charged with meaning," to borrow Eliot's phrase. Literature is made up of language finely or coarsely attuned to the substance of the work and closely patterned to convey that substance. Complaints about the language—especially the dialogue—of Eugene O'Neill are justified because, among other things, his characters are not endowed with language fine enough or rich enough to evoke the depths of the experience with which he sets out to deal. And it seems to be no accident that one of the richest, most complex, and most highly individualized portraits in modern fiction in English—that of Stephen Dedalus, in *A Portrait of the Artist as a Young Man*—is by one of modern literature's great magicians of language. One element in the *Portrait* is Joyce's finely reticulated pulling in of allusive material at precisely the moments when it can heighten our responsiveness and deepen our insight into Stephen's conscious and unconscious life.

The unconscious life is a crucial element. Insofar as characters in literature are constructed on the pattern of people in life, and insofar as we assume that people in life have unconscious motives, we must assume that we can legitimately form hypotheses about the unconscious springs of their actions. Language is a key element in this, as is the imagery for which language is the vehicle. I have shown elsewhere that part of the exquisite craftsmanship of *A Portrait of the Artist as a Young Man* lies in its evocation, through language and imagery, of the patterns of identification that define Stephen's identity, from earliest infancy, when he identifies with Baby Tuckoo in the story "his father told him" to the moment at the very end of the novel, when he clinches his identification with Icarus, not Daedalus. These patterns provide not only the scaffolding on which we construct an understanding of his character but also the configuration of issues on which the novel's whole thematic structure finally rests.[15]

The fact that the dimensions and levels of Stephen's

character are embedded in language dramatizes the extent to which Stephen exists "only" in language and the complexity of the critical acts that we perform when we extricate him from the language of the novel. This, of course, is the paradox that launched me on the last leg of my discourse—the paradox of utter embeddedness and radical detachability. The Stephen whose unconscious conflicts we anatomize is a Stephen who has been "liberated" from his text, yet his most unconscious and perhaps decisive motives are coded into the most deeply bound elements of the text—namely, the words that constitute it.

Language, of course, works in still more obvious ways. Everything we know about characters in narratives, and most of what we know about them in drama, is conveyed in words. We infiltrate the consciousnesses of characters directly and indirectly, through the language they use and the language others use about them. These others include characters who speak about them in dramas and stories, as well as narrators privileged to tell us what the characters think and feel. The latter often use, with varying degrees of "fidelity," the very language and imagery that the characters themselves might use. Indeed, the "inward turn of narrative" in the novel has rested largely on the invention of ever more subtle means of revealing inwardness.[16]

The language used by the characters themselves is one of the traditional means of distinguishing them from each other and of distinguishing each one in him- or herself. Such characterization has been in the forefront of critical consciousness since the time of the classical rhetoricians, but it often operates more subtly than merely "characteristic" speech. Indeed, sometimes the particularization of a character through his or her language is effective not because it is idiosyncratically (or "idiolectically") appropriate, but rather because of its highly stylized rhetoricity or its marked stereotypicality. Paradoxically, in such characters the intensification of banality generates the sense that someone particular is "there," speaking it. Orsino, in the opening speech of *Twelfth Night*, is generated in this way; so, in another sense, is Othello throughout much of his text. Orsino does not exist so much "in himself" or in his "own" language as in something (we call it poetry) that is precipitated out of the field of possibilities in the verbal texture of the work that generates him.

A massive heaping up of words, often of markedly mauled or eroded words, is a tried-and-true device of satiric and ironic texts, but its by-product is often character. The scholastic disputants of *Gargantua and Pantagruel* are such characters; so, in a weird way, are Flaubert's Bouvard and Pécuchet; Falstaff, slippery and vital "tub of guts" though he is, may be another, with his flamboyant wrenching of logic and language. What happens in each of these vastly different instances is that a recognizable rhetorical mode is elaborated to the point where a character emerges, often with the aid of actions and gestures wholly congruous with his or her speech. Such gestures are felt to be a mechanical extension of speech. This happens, of course, in life as well; we recognize the Miss Bateses of the world by the fact that their speech seems to be made up of nothing but bumbling circumlocution. The characters who are created through the exploitation of such language are generated by the entire verbal medium of the work, which heightens and amplifies the conventional material in hand and facets it within the configuration of the text in such a way as to heighten its resonance—until a figure emerges, apparently *ex vacuo*, from words, without meaning-fraught action.

The rhetorical character of the field in which characters are generated manifests itself in still other curious and characteristic ways. In a superb essay on *Othello*, Antoinette B. Dauber suggests that Desdemona is generated at the meeting point, or collision point, of two kinds of rhetoric; an idealizing rhetoric, which reached its self-conscious peak in Spenser but figures unselfconsciously in the speech of Othello and Cassio, and an ironic mode of discourse that receives its ultimate reductive apotheosis in Iago.[17] Dauber does not fully develop the implications of her analysis for the characters, but it seems to me that one could say that Desdemona is created as a kind of shimmer or spume at the point where the antithetical rhetorics meet. She speaks and acts in the play, but in the end we apprehend her chiefly in the field of interpretation that Othello, Cassio, Iago, and others create for her. Hence she can be seen on the one hand as an illusion arising at the meeting point of rhetorical modes and on the other as a reality around which the rhetoric is precipitated.

A further and no less arcane function of language can be seen in texts where the entire verbal texture of the work is highly accommodated to the consciousness, sensibility, or meaning of a particular character. The humor of *Great Expectations* is not Pip's but Dickens', but the humor and the verbal manipulations that generate the humor of the twenty-odd introductory chapters of the novel are a generating medium for Pip. Pip exists as he is for us largely because of the quaint comic incongruities of language, exploiting the situations through which he is projected. Similarly in Faulkner's "Barn Burning," although the narrative voice tells us much that Sarty does not know, the Faulknerian verbal surge serves to objectify his bewilderment. Technically, we say that much of the story is focalized through Sarty (or, in *Great Expectations*, through Pip). But the very language in which we see what Sarty sees, as well as the language in which we see and come to understand other things, bears on Sarty and serves to generate Sarty.

I seem to be again propounding a paradox. Having held that characters can be liberated from the language that generates them, I am now saying that they can be generated almost exclusively by language functioning as sheer language, and not only as the medium for rendering characteristic modes of behavior. Yet this paradox is only a further aspect of the preceding one—that characters are utterly embedded in texts and absolutely detachable from them.

So far I have chosen to exemplify Homo Fictus largely in terms of characters who figure in literary structures that confer a considerable measure of autonomy and detachability upon them. Such characters—Edgar, in *King Lear,* is a singular exception—tend to stand either at the center of a work or at the center of a relatively autonomous segment of a work. I have focused on such characters with a view to exemplifying in the least complicated way how the specifically literary organization of texts generates the formal and substantive schemas that sustain characters. To linger too long with such characters, who are for the most part more or less minimally stylized in their mode of presentation and relatively coherent, transparent, and dynamic as well, is to distort the overall picture of character in literature. The kind of characters I have been discussing are probably the minority among characters in literature, and so are the texts that generate them. But they are useful here not only for what they exemplify in themselves but for purposes of contrast with other kinds of characters, who are major and central, but less autonomous than they.

The distinguishing marks of an Elizabeth Bennet, for example, are not solely the relative realism of her presentation and the impression of complexity and coherence of her personality but also the fact that she is defined in terms of a discreteness that is possibly unique to her type of literary figure. What I mean is that although the women in *Pride and Prejudice* are all analogues of Elizabeth, none of them should be seen as a fragment or a projection of her. Within the surface structure of the text, at least, Elizabeth is herself alone, capable of developing—but not of being transformed— into a person who has some of the qualities of the other people in the novel; yet she is never collapsible into any one of them. *Pride and Prejudice* centers on Elizabeth, and its patterning of characters, images, and relationships illuminates her. Nothing from her surrounding world leaks into her character, however, except by means of her perceiving consciousness and experiencing self. She and her consciousness depend on the whole text, but they possess an ample autonomy within it. This relative autonomy is one of the things she has in common with people in life.

This is much less the case with other types of character, beginning with those who inhabit the kind of narrative that Northrop Frye calls romance, and that he contrasts with what he calls novels. His primary example of the novel is *Pride and Prejudice;* of the romance, *Wuthering Heights.* The romance, as I understand it, projects characters who are at least as vivid and coherent, and initially as stable, as Elizabeth Bennet or King Lear, but who are in the end less autonomous and less detachable. They also are more dependent for their meaning on a global configuration of characters, situations, and images than their counterparts in novels and (in the drama) those in such tragedies as *King Lear.*

The romance, in Frye's definition, "does not attempt to create 'real people' so much as stylized figures which expand into psychological archetypes. It is in the romance that we find Jung's libido, anima and shadow reflected in the hero, heroine and villain."[18] I don't know that the Jungian archetypes are useful or appropriate here, but it is true that in certain kinds of narratives (and romance, as Frye defines it, is one of them) the characters are not radically discrete but rather interpenetrate and even fuse with each other, forming part of a single psychic or spiritual pattern. Thus we can isolate Catherine from Heathcliff and Heathcliff from Catherine and speak of each of them as a separate character. Indeed, for many purposes we must do this. Beyond a certain point, however, we must speak in terms of a psychic reciprocity, even a symbiosis, between them. Catherine says, "Anyone who separates us will meet the fate of Milo," and there is a level at which they are envisioned as one thing, like "the eternal rocks beneath." The same is true of Hester, Dimmesdale, and Chillingworth in *The Scarlet Letter.* We can and must think of them separately, but finally, to make real sense of them and of the novel they inhabit, we must think of them as an elusive ensemble of psychic qualities that form a composite of something: not necessarily of a person, but of a psychic state and a moral pattern.

Even in works not dramatically marked as romance—and Frye makes the point that all modes are mixed, that there are no "pure" examples of any literary type—we see this phenomenon. In *David Copperfield*, for example, Steerforth and Uriah Heep finally make sense only as projections of David. Indeed, the whole incoherent series of seductions and attempted seductions in the novel's tangled plot can be made final sense of only if we see their perpetrators as projections that can be pulled back into the configuration of David's rather tenuous inner life.

In romance the substantive issues are as complex as in the novel, and the characters are initially as coherent, but each character is less complex in and for itself, and less highly faceted. This is the case despite the complexity of the spiritual and psychic issues projected through such characters. It is also true despite the fact that in works that fuse novel and romance elements—for example *Crime and Punishment*— we sometimes have characters more vividly complex than novels ordinarily generate. As for ordinary romance characters, they are often more coherent, monolithic, and stable—at least for considerable stretches of the action—than the more self-contained and less stylized characters of the novel and of tragedy. This combination of relative simplicity and extreme initial sharpness of definition probably has to do with the fact that, as Frye says, the romance is closer to the unconscious life, radiating from and cleaving more closely to the world of dreams. This is why, as Frye puts it, "romance . . . often radiates a glow of subjective intensity."[19] In romance, people are driven, rather than conscious; coerced, rather than struggling volitionally to achieve ends that their conscious selves affirm.

The paradigmatic difference between an Elizabeth as heroine of a novel and a Catherine Earnshaw as heroine of a romance lies in the fact that Elizabeth impresses us as a person in whom the play of consciousness and will is considerable, and whose consciousness is poised to field a great variety of impressions and impulses. Elizabeth must exert her will in the light of what she learns; she must make decisions and act on them. The challenge for an Elizabeth is to weave together all the strands of her experience and to integrate them into the pattern of her life and personality, as she would want them to be. The field of Catherine's consciousness is narrowed to the givens of her personality, and she struggles to maintain those givens in a rather static way. She resists change and development, clinging to the familiar elements of her experience. Catherine exerts her will, but she wills only those things that magnetize the field of her imperious subjectivity. The limits to her willing are the limits of her personality but also are aspects of her symbiosis with Heathcliff.

The difference between these two kinds of character— between Elizabeth Bennet and Catherine Earnshaw—can be illuminated by a distinction that we make in life and that bears upon still other types of character as well. Again, Homo Sapiens illuminates Homo Fictus. As I noted earlier, in life we assume people to be coherent, and we also assume that each individual undergoes a process of development and maturation that moves toward the largest possible integration of needs and feelings into the functioning of the conscious self. The protagonists of hero-centered realistic novels and normative tragedies approximate, in greater and lesser degrees, some such model. The catastrophe in tragedies is often brought about by a lapse from such integration under the stress of circumstance or feeling. In practice, however, people in life achieve only relative and very different degrees of integration, and characters in literature need not necessarily be subject to it at all.

Both Elizabeth and Catherine are subject to criteria of coherence but in very different ways. Within the limits of possibility established by *Pride and Prejudice*, Elizabeth manifests an ever-expanding consciousness of herself, or Darcy, and of her world, and she remains true to herself as she integrates what she knows within what she is. In the terms established by *Wuthering Heights*, Catherine strives for a synthesis of possibilities, in life and in consciousness, but achieves no such thing. Her death merely consummates the substance of her life; in her postmortem existence she continues to enact the single tension that animated her in life. The meaning of both characters depends on their place within the whole field of meaning created by the novels that generate them. But Catherine depends more completely on the supporting figuration of the whole novel for that meaning and for our sense of her existence.

As a character in a romance, Catherine squints two ways. On the one hand, she is related to her analogues in novels, such characters as Elizabeth, whom we identify as themselves and whose coherence we perceive directly. On the other hand, Catherine's simplified, unselfconscious, compulsive, and coerced identity looks toward another kind of figure that is more native to romance: the double. Indeed, insofar as Catherine is twinned with Heathcliff, she may be said to be his double. More thoroughgoing double figures, however, have a far more radical lack of autonomy, a more definitive lack of existence in themselves. The double *is* the shadow, the fragmented piece of imagined identity, embodied in a figure who appears in fiction as a separate person. As with Catherine and Heathcliff, each fragment may have definable traits, coherence, and identity. But neither fragment makes a viable whole without the other, and the two together depend on the entire configuration of images in the work for meaning.[20]

In life, the reading of doubles points to the splitting of real personalities; Otto Rank read them thus and read literary doubles in the light of them.[21] So have most other interpreters of the phenomenon. In life, doubling means fragmentation of the self, a disruption of its coherence. In literature it may be related to still more fundamental rupturing of coherence in character. As I noted at the beginning of this chapter, there is no reason for characters in literature to be generated within the terms of the hypothetical coherence we assume for people in life. Characters in literature, as I have been insisting, have no real life histories and often no imagined ones; they often provide no data to explain the grounds of consistency or coherence within themselves, coherence that might account for their behavior. In varying degrees, and for various reasons, characters often provide us with no ways of explaining their behavior—for motivating it, in human terms. The reasons for the absence of such grounds of motivation can range from the most rudimentary sloppiness in tying up the loose ends of an action to the most sophisticated manipulation of rhetorical surfaces (as with Shakespeare's Troilus and Cressida and Nabokov's Sebastian Knight) with a view to obstructing interpretation or dramatizing the factitiousness or the tenuousness of the characters themselves.

The cases of neglect, sloppiness, or artistic failure are easy to locate. Such problems crop up in the work of even the most accomplished creators of coherent characters, such as Shakespeare or George Eliot. Clearly there are no significant data about Edmund's life to help us make psychological sense of his deathbed recantation and his revelation of his plan to kill Lear and Cordelia. Nor is there much ground for exploring why Dorothea Brooke loses the tension and complexity of her being once Casaubon is dead. In fact, it is a common perception—Forster formulates it tellingly in *Aspects of the Novel*—that even characters who seem intended to suggest real people are often warped to meet the needs of the plot.[22] Maggie Tulliver or Euripides' Medea may be given scope for being, feeling, and growing in the course of a work's unfolding, and then be pinched back into relative nullity as the action winds down to a close. With such characters we may reach for underlying unity and for the logic of the developments, or lack of them. But we may often find ourselves in a life-historical or motivational dead end. The same is true of characters who are not wrenched to point a moral or resolve a tale but who miscarry in the course of their presentation,

like James's Hyacinth Robinson or, possibly, Shakespeare's
Timon of Athens.

It would be a dire mistake, however, to limit the treatment of incoherence in character to the miscarriage of particular works or even to consistent conventions that open the
way for large gaps in motivation or consciousness. To deal
with character in literature in its largest scope, we must find
a place for all kinds of characters, including/those conceived
within the terms of highly self-reflexive works whose metapoetic
interest dictates the generation of characters who are purely
functional and whose functionality is underscored within the
work./We have, moreover, to find ways of dealing with
characters whose creators deliberately highlight the rhetoricity
of their being and therefore permit no consecutive, coherent,
or exhaustive reading of their substance or motives. To the
first group belong such characters as Signor Hirsch in Conrad's
Nostromo and Silbermann in *The Real Life of Sebastian Knight*;[23]
to the second, such figures as Rameau's Nephew, who enacts,
in his lack of coherent identity, the theme of the work that
bears his name. Shakespeare's Troilus and Cressida are conceived in a similar way, to stress the rhetoricity of their
being, so that we are hard put to determine which traits
belong to them and which to the literary traditions from
which Shakespeare took them.[24]
   At the opposite end of the scale, operating in no less
interesting ways, are characters whose motivation is so simple,
so transparent, so "transitive," as almost to elude explication.
Such characters belong to the type I briefly discussed in
chapter 1—Todorov's "narrative men," whose being is an
attribute of the actions they perform. Among such narrative
men Todorov enumerates the characters of *The Arabian Nights*
and of most folktales.[25]
   Since literature is full of dramatically incoherent, inconsistent,
and opaque characters, as well as of coherent, consistent, and
transparent ones, it has an elaborate system of signposting, of

indicating the generic and substantive concerns of its various texts and of cluing us in on how to take the various characters within them. Life—society, culture, institutions—has analogous systems, as when it tells us that enemies or slaves are not as human as we are and deflects the possibility of our identifying with them, or when it conditions doctors not to identify with patients lest their professional competence be impaired. The signs that literature provides are different. The signs that narrative uses are, to begin with, uniformly verbal and on the whole fairly explicit. And they tend to be still more highly, even compulsively, organized than their analogues in life. Because of this system of signs in literature, we must acknowledge, even if we accept Chatman's view as to the need for an "open" theory of character, that openness, like coherence or complexity, depends on the nature of the text in which it appears—that is, on its substantive and generic signposting. For all literary texts, even as they invite us to imagine some things, effectively prevent us from imagining others. They do so by blocking off possible avenues of vision. We can blast through such barriers, but we do so at a price.

Thus, a fairy tale by definition avoids giving us more of Cinderella or her wicked stepsisters than we need for the sake of the story. Of the stepsisters we need see only their selfishness, spitefulness, and greed. To attribute any motive beyond ravening ambition to the act of cutting off heel or toe in this story is to go beyond the signifying structures of the text. We may have motives of our own for accepting the self-mutilation as possible and real, and the text as a whole, as Bruno Bettelheim has shown, may suggest fantasies of which self-mutilation is an integral part.[26] But these motives and fantasies cannot be attributed to the characters. In contrast, a realistic novel invites us to speculate on motives and to bring a considerable range of our own fantasies and experience to bear on its interpretation. Emma Bovary dresses in male attire only at certain moments, but the whole pattern of her presentation—the structure of signs that generates her—suggests a possibility for going behind the details of presentation to extrapolate a psychologically concrete motive for her doing so.[27] Stephen Dedalus, peering into his mother's mirror during a crisis of writing, actively invites us to speculate on his motives and on the unconscious meaning of the action.

In the spectrum of fiction ranging between fairy tale and realistic novel, there is a large variety of modes (for example, fable, satire, Theophrastan "character," and comedy of manners) that invite us to envision their characters in terms of different depths and complexities of motivation. These depths and complexities are signified within the generic signposting of the work as a whole.

Generic definition is relative, of course. Since Harold Bloom began to speak of the "anxiety of influence," a submerged truth has moved to the center of our consciousness—namely, that even in epochs when writers strove to emulate classical models, the "imitation" of those models was never slavish but took the form of incessant modification and re-creation of existing modes. In emulating classical forms, writers of substance have always transformed their models.[28] To work within a genre is to adapt that genre to the needs of the present moment and the present will. Hence even when there are no wildly anomalous things in a work to interfere with the smooth movement of an accepted convention—as, for example, when the full weight of Shylock's experience intrudes upon the romance of *The Merchant of Venice*—the new work reshapes the old convention.

People still argue about whether Shylock "got out of hand," or whether Shakespeare deliberately skewed his generic model by jamming Shylock into it, or whether we just don't know how to "read" the attitude to Shylock implied by the play as a whole. Whichever view is true, it is clear that Shakespeare has done something to his model and that the usual signals for "reading" character and meaning are somewhat obscured. Barabbas, Marlowe's Jew of Malta, who is

clearly Shylock's model, similarly exists in a play that strad-
dles the kindred genres of melodrama and farce with a gleam
of human substance and intellectual challenge that belies
them both. Silas Marner is likewise an amphibious being,
subsisting within a work that integrates fairy tale with realistic psychological motivation at both the psychological and the
narrative levels. Less dramatically (and less successfully),
Raffles stands out within *Middlemarch* not chiefly as a Dickensian
intrusion, as most critics would have it, but as a character
whose singleness of motive jars on a reader who has been
conditioned to live with the other denizens of the *Middlemarch*
world and with the novel's conception of mixed motives and
slow, grinding erosion of personalities.

Most readers will agree that Raffles is a catastrophe, both as
a character and as a part of the fabric that is *Middlemarch*. In
principle, however, generic mixing or superimposition provides one of the primary fields for generating character. I
have already noted the impression of complexity that
Dostoevsky achieves in his fusion of novel and romance.
Similarly, the nineteenth-century novel can be said to achieve
some of its more complex effects by combining an essentially
comic plot with a protagonist who is viewed with the sympathy that we extend to a tragic figure. If we perceive this, we
may have some additional perspective on the peculiar vibran-
cy that informs the protagonists of such novels.[29] The shimmer of "iridescence of a personality" such as Gwendolyn
Harleth's (and the phrase is George Eliot's, coined for
Gwendolyn) derives partly from the disparate literary and
generic materials that go into her fabrication—the legendary,
romantic, and novelistic figurations that beget her. Just as the
linguistic texture of *A Portrait of the Artist as a Young Man*
pulls in all kinds of associations and elaborations of Stephen's
"being," so its generic texture—like that of *Daniel Deronda* or,
in varying degrees, any other novel—incorporates elements
of various modes to fabricate a Stephen. In contrast, Kafka's
bewilderingly minimal story "Eleven Sons" neutralizes the
possibility of conceiving of characters by playing off the

reader's expectation that each of the sons will have qualities all his own against the expectation established in the text as it unfolds that no one can have any definable qualities at all.[30]

The range of possibilities within generic mixing is not our concern here, however. The point I wish to establish is that the formal, structural, and generic elements of literary texts serve in characteristically literary ways to generate images of characters and that the images depend on the characteristic literary quality of the texts for their generation. Characters in their kinds are generated by texts in their kinds.

4

Characters in Their Kinds:
A Taxonomy

My argument, again, is that although we necessarily read
Homo Fictus in terms of Homo Sapiens, they are not
identical, and Homo Fictus must be confronted in terms
appropriate to him. To "read" him aright, we must acknowledge the context in which he is generated and find modes of
discourse appropriate to his nature as denizen of a literary
text.

This is doubly important because the genres to which
many of us are habituated, such as the novel and realistic
drama, tend to project characters constructed in such a way
as to suggest a coherence, a wholeness, a complexity, a
dynamism, and an existence in the past, present, and future—
that is, a life history—closely analogous to that of real
people. Even in the novel and the realistic drama, however,
we encounter characters who are not even superficially
verisimilar. Moreover, even when the protagonist of a novel is
presented realistically as a dynamic, developing character to
whose feelings we have access, the other characters, as John
Harvey notes, are often conceived in a very different way.[1]

This fact constitutes a major problem for Harvey, as I
observe in chapter 2. If we perceive verisimilar characters as
"like life" and read them in terms of their resemblance to

living people, how are we to conceptualize characters who are neither lifelike nor like life? To deal with this question, Harvey complicates E. M. Forster's polarization of characters in literature into flat ones and round ones in an interesting, though to my mind ultimately inadequate, way. Harvey, discussing character in the novel, enumerates not two but four types of characters: (1) the protagonist; (2) the card; (3) the choric character; (4) the *ficelle*.[2] The "protagonist" is meant to be like us and is seen from many vantage points, in many situations, so that many facets and possibilities are revealed within his or her personality. In this sense the protagonist is normally quite "round." The "card," on the other hand, is an intensified, wildly energized, animated, often caricaturistic or grotesque version of a person—an active and sometimes galvanic version of Forster's flat figures. The function of the card (as was noted in chapter 2 with regard to all secondary characters) is to support and illuminate the main character. Harvey calls such characters "cards" because they are often odd or outrageous and take dealing with.

Choric characters and *ficelles* are almost wholly functional, engaging us not on the grounds of their own qualities but in terms of what they communicate about the world projected in the text. The *ficelle*, as Henry James defines it, is a character who serves to set off, contrast with, dramatize, and engage the protagonist, as "foils" in drama traditionally do.[3] The choric character serves not so much to define a character other than him- or herself as to define an environment, a theme, or a mode of response; Harvey notes that Hardy's rustics are a classic example. In Harvey's view, all three noncentral character types (card, *ficelle*, and choric character) serve to generate the complex network of relationships that is the world of the novel and that puts us in the desired perceptual and moral relation to the protagonist, whose nature, conflicts, and experience are, according to Harvey, the novel's raison d'être.[4]

Harvey's analysis of the function of secondary and

nonmimetic characters in the economy of the novel's moral teleology is trenchant and useful, but it is also problematic. The two supplementary categories of the choric character and the *ficelle* identify functions that characters can fill but say little or nothing about the substance of such characters or about their modes of being. Nor do these categories apply to characters in genres less mimetic than the novel.

Any adequate account of character in literature must try to define the various aspects and modes of such characters' existence both in themselves and within the texts that generate them. Such definition must isolate a range of qualities inherent in characters, and that range must be much wider than Forster's single polarity of "flat" and "round" and still more comprehensive than the scheme that Harvey provides. It must allow for a considerable range of characteristics, on a scale that permits a wide spectrum of possibilities within each category. The spectrum must be wide enough to encompass the whole range of possibilities in literature. It must include characters who seem to simulate how people appear to us at their most complex, dynamic, and accessible and also characters who, as I noted in my second chapter, evoke the way people seem to us when they flit and flicker across the pageant of our lives or when they crop up in our paranoias— or our dreams. It must be rich and flexible enough, moreover, to allow characters to be transposed, when we find it useful to transpose them, into modes appropriate to other kinds of character, as I suggest in chapter 2. The nightmare Quilp and the driven Svidrigaylov, for example, should be translatable into more transparent, more realistically motivated characters than they in fact are. But before we transpose them into whatever mode we choose, for whatever purpose we may have, we must be able to describe them as they are, both in themselves and in the total economy of the works that generate them.

In fact, any adequate view of character must take into account a fairly large range of qualities and possibilities. To meet this need, I propose a sequence of eight categories that describe aspects of characters in literature, categories that allow us to conceptualize the images we form of such characters as we "liberate" them from the texts within which they figure.[5] For each of these categories moreover, I propose its polar opposite. The categories that I propose and their opposites, are:

Stylization	Naturalism
Coherence	Incoherence
Wholeness	Fragmentariness
Literalness	Symbolism
Complexity	Simplicity
Transparency	Opacity
Dynamism	Staticism
Closure	Openness

Each of the categories, with its opposite, defines the extreme end of a scale on which we can place characters in literature. Together the categories allow us to define the qualities of specific characters in literature and specific groups of characters with some accuracy, and, when necessary or desirable, with some exhaustiveness.

In what follows I shall define each category both in itself and in terms of its antithesis, exemplifying each with characters that lend themselves to analysis in its terms. The aspects of character dealt with in each category tend to dovetail with aspects implied by others, so that the categories tend to imply each other. Not all aspects are equally relevant to all characters, but no character, it seems to me, can be defined in and for itself without consideration of each of them.

Stylization

Stylization seems to be the simplest but also the most elusive of my categories. It is also the most comprehensive, constituting a kind of umbrella category, one that bears on almost all of the others that follow. Yet it seems to me to be necessary, and distinguishable from the others.

Stylization is a familiar term that is easy to exemplify. I think we know exactly what is meant when we are told that Anna Karenina is less stylized in presentation than Catherine Earnshaw and that Catherine Earnshaw is less stylized than Estella in *Great Expectations*, while Estella is still less stylized than Miss Havisham. What these examples suggest, I think, is the fact that stylization has to do with some model or norm from which stylized characterizations deviate. The norm, in the sequence of examples that I bring, is clearly resemblance to real people, which means some form of realism or naturalism of representation. After all, when we say that something is stylized, we mean that we can define the original, or the raw material, or the norm that is deformed or reformed in the course of its creation. That something must be *there* before it can be shaped to a greater or lesser degree in its re-presentation.

Hence the difficulty of the term. What do we mean when we speak of the "originals" or "models" of the figures presented in literature? As I have already noted, characters in literature are not and cannot be transcriptions or even re-presentations of people who exist, although in inception, conception, or intention they may (even in considerable part) be that too. They are constructions of creatures who might exist or at least may be imagined, as conceived in whatever terms the writer and the writer's culture conceive of people and other kinds of agents—vegetable, mineral, animal, or even divine. As E. H. Gombrich has shown, the criteria of verisimilitude— of correlation or congruity between a representation of an object and the object that it purports to represent—vary from age to age and from culture to culture.[6]

The difficulty is real but not insuperable. In a general way, we share quite a clear notion of what we mean by an unstylized image of a person. Our conception of people whom we live and work with is essentially not stylized but naturalistic. Historically, I think the normative image of the human being, from the Renaissance to the early twentieth century, is the realistic portrait, as reflected in painted portraits from, say, Holbein and Van Eyck to Cézanne and Van

Gogh. In literary rather than visual terms, this means the presentation in texts of the qualities of individuals—their appearance, actions, thoughts, responses, aspirations—in terms that approximate the normative expectations of self-manifestation in life. Such portraiture, it seems to me, is more a substantive than a formal procedure, although certain formal elements seem native and necessary to it.

The kind of naturalistic literary representation I am speaking of assumes that people operate exclusively in the natural world, within an essentially historical horizon, and that they can conceive of the objects they are striving for in fairly definite terms. The terms, to be sure, may be transcendent as well as naturalistic, as J. Leeds Barroll convincingly shows in dealing with Shakespeare.[7] The objects of striving, however, even when transcendent, are presented in concrete, usually visible, psychologically explicable terms. Indeed, much of the naturalistic literary portraiture of the period from, say, 1500 to 1914 depends on the vivid evocation of such objects of striving either through the objectified world presented in a work or through the field of reference generated by its language. For one of the major instruments of naturalistic portraiture is validation of the striver, as subject, by representation of the object of his or her striving—the object of the character's desire or loathing. The vividness of Anna Karenina's presentation, for example, depends to a considerable extent on the vividness of presentation of the Karenin she flees and the Vronsky she loves; of the Levin who symbolically might serve as her fulfillment; and then of the Vronsky whose limitedness evokes the narcissism that is the source of her doom. In addition, high naturalistic portraiture from, say, Shakespeare and Cervantes to Proust and Joyce assumes a significant affinity between character and world, even when the character—a Clarissa Harlowe or a Julien Sorel—comes to transcend her or his world.

Such portraiture, moreover, assumes that people are complex and subject to rending conflict. That is, it assumes more or less what Keats assumes in his sonnet on *King Lear* (see chapter 2) and what I take to be the norm for our conceptualization of people in literature and in life. Indeed, such portraiture assumes that people are so complex and so torn by inner conflict that they often seem discontinuous. But the tradition also assumes that however discontinuous a character appears to be—as with Lear, before his madness and after it, or with Othello, who is first seen as a masterfully composed warrior and then as a rabidly jealous husband—there is an underlying continuity, as there is underlying coherence in any person in life. Though the nature and consistency of any individual's identity may constitute a problem, as Hume argued and as postmodernist fiction insists, the prevailing image of human beings, as attested by the classic literature of our civilization from the Renaissance to the first decades of our century, tends to circumvent that problem by positing the existence of some underlying unity.

In our Freudian age we tend, as I noted in chapter 2, to affirm a dynamic psychology postulating a unity in tension between the conscious and the unconscious life and between the play of conflicting motives in the conscious life. The Freudian view, however, as Freud himself acknowledged, is a culmination of the entire Renaissance and post-Renaissance tradition. The tradition assumes the existence of a mysterious underlife in the self and strives to evoke or to explicate it. The tradition also assumes a complex dialectical interplay between the apparent coherence of the formed person and the manifold potential incoherence of the underself.

Another way of speaking of the normative view of the human being from the Renaissance to at least the first third of our century is to say that the conception that prevails is a highly individualizing one, if not always an individualistic one in the classical sense. People are thought of as potentially, if not always actually, unique. Each is a nonpareil, either in his or her given nature or in the self he or she struggles to actualize. That tendency to isolate and portray what is individual and unique in every person has led to an effort to give us images of people as they are, not as they ought to be.

It also tends to present them, as I have already said, in terms of the engagement of their wills and self-images with the world. That world is the world we live in, more or less as it is apprehended in consciousness.

So far I have used the term *naturalistic portraiture* as a convenient phrase to describe the opposite of stylized representation of people. Since there can in fact be no "natural" —that is, nonconventionalized—reflection of whatever it is we think of as "natural," it might be useful to adopt less misleading terms. Hence I propose from this point on to work with a scale of stylization running from minimal to maximal and to use the term *minimal stylization* to describe more or less naturalistic portraiture. More accurately, minimal stylization involves the depiction of characters in more or less normative terms and in terms of the way we naturally might perceive them if they really existed. Again, I say "minimal" stylization, rather than "no" stylization because clearly any organized presentation of a set of traits and motives, however naturalistic in manner, involves an organizing and shaping that necessarily constitute a kind of stylization, implicit in the schematization of the material. Ordinarily there is also a heightening of what is "given" in the normative conception of character with which a writer works. Hence the frequent presence of more than minimal stylization in most relatively naturalistic characterizations. Such stylization is reflected in the purely verbal style of texts, as well as in their formal modes of portrayal. Heightening of language in Shakespeare, as the vehicle for vivid representation of the inner life as well as for the telescoping of qualities and motives to the point of stereoscopy, are typical of the process. So is the use of symbolic fields of externalized, "expressionist" events, as in the scene with the blind beggar at the end of *Madame Bovary.*

Because of the vital need for such stylization, the artifice of apparent nonstylization involved in apparent inarticulateness or the sort of subliterate, pseudocolloquial expressionism found, for example, in O'Neill's dialogue are fallings away from the high achievement of Renaissance and post-Renaissance portraiture. Conditioned by that achievement, we are prone to feel that such minimal stylization, such slice-of-life notation of how people "really" look and speak, violates the reality of people as they are. Indeed, Beckett's curiously reductive rendering of people, experience, and consciousness is a reductio ad absurdum—a highly stylized parody—of this mode; Beckett draws directly on what Joyce did in the parodic sequences of *Ulysses* and *Finnegans Wake* and on Flaubert's mocking parrotry in *Bouvard et Pécuchet*.

The range of what I call *minimal stylization* is considerable. If we use Northrop Frye's division of fiction into five modes— mythic, romantic, high mimetic, low mimetic, and ironic—we find that both high and low mimetic, and part of the ironic mode as well, fall into the range of minimal stylization.[8] From the vantage point of character conceptions, both the high and low mimetic modes are characterized by a marked emphasis on the unity, wholeness, strivingness, and at least the potential and partial presentation of consciousness of the characters. Forster's round characters, as he describes them, are within a convention of minimal stylization. So are the kinds of characters Frye speaks of as typical of the novel as opposed to the romance, the encyclopedic forms, and Menippean satire—that is, the kind of characters who inhabit normative social worlds with distinctive codes of manners and morality. Although such characters are generated within conventions native to the genres and periods that nurture them, we come to envision them as individualized, conflict-ridden, relatively unified or coherent beings.

Maximal stylization, on the other hand, figures in the projection of the caricaturistic grotesques who tend to be Forster's "flat" characters and Harvey's "cards." That is, they are—if we assume that we possess some norm for perceiving a person as we conventionally conceive people to be—harsh intensifications and often simplifications of "natural" people. James's *ficelle* may well become highly stylized; the redoubtable Henrietta Stackpole in the formally realistic though highly mannered mode of *The Portrait of a Lady* often figures as a grotesque, as does Mrs. Touchett, with her touches of satire and romance. In the realistic novel, of the sort that George Eliot writes, such characters as Raffles in *Middlemarch* and Bob Jakin in *The Mill on the Floss* are rendered with more stylization than Bulstrode and Maggie. In Dickens, whose novels represent a fantastic, satiric variation on the normative realistic novel, Miss Havisham is more stylized than Pip, and Wemmick is in some ways still more stylized than Miss Havisham, even as Jaggers is more stylized than Wemmick.

In all of these instances, minimal and maximal stylization of character involves manipulation of conventional norms for characterization. The norms include a considerable range of possibilities, many of which are related to genre. Thus, although caricature and the grotesque dictate one extreme mode of stylization, pastoral and romantic conventions dictate another, milder kind of distortion of the post-Renaissance norm for character. The norms of less than maximal stylization dictate the depiction of innocents, such as Tom Jones or the Heros and Rosalinds of Shakespeare's pleasant comedies. This is a relatively limited, nongrotesque kind of stylization, involving an extreme tepidness and absence of personal coloration. Hence although these characters do not manifest formal, caricaturistic distortion, they lack both character and personality in the ordinary sense. Such characters necessarily figure as *simple* (as opposed to *complex*, another pair of terms in my taxonomy), and the characters who fall into this category also tend to be simple—even simpletons—in the common sense of the term.

The creatures of pastoral romance, to which some of Shakespeare's "pleasant" heroines to some limited extent belong, are still more simple. Their characterizations, if we evaluate them in terms of the conventions of the genres to which they belong, are also more stylized. More highly stylized still are the figures who populate the allegorical masques in Shakespeare's plays; think of Ceres, in the masque in *The Tempest*, who has already figured in my discourse.

Such characters have minimal personal, psychological, and imaginative existence for us, being subject, from the vantage point of naturalistic portraiture, to a lethal blandness, a deadly lack of reflexive or other consciousness, and a devastating absence of mediated and mediating will. Yet they figure in coherent sequences that often have a power and enchantment of their own. The power and magic of the masques hinge on the subordination of character to other purposes in the play and involve (to anticipate other key terms) absence of conflict, total coherence, and lack of access to inwardness—an inwardness that clearly does not and cannot exist for these characters.

In Shakespeare such simplification gives rise to the highly stylized, fragmentary, and grotesque characters who abound in his work, characters that, though incomplete, are not simple. Caliban is an excellent example, as is Puck, and so are many of the fools, including the Fool in *King Lear.* These are creatures who epitomize some dimension of experience or some term of a polarity being played out in the work. Such experience and such polarity are ordinarily explicable and integratable in terms of the experience of the character(s) at the center of the play, in exactly the same way as cards, in Harvey's view, explicate the experience of the heroes of the novels they figure in. In the novel, extreme cases of flanking explicatory figures are to be found in the blind beggar in *Madame Bovary* and his kinsman, the little peasant with the hammer in Anna Karenina's dreams. They are also related to the kind of projection of psychic qualities that Frye finds in novelistic romance, with the difference that they cluster around the less stylized characters of what Frye calls the novel, figures to whose responses and consciousness we are given greater and more rationalized access.

It will be noted that the whole range of stylization must include all degrees of simplification, attenuation, schematization, and grotesquification. A general view of character must encompass the whole range of characters that literature includes and must deal with them in all of their manifestations, including those that appear to represent utterly dehumanized human figures or nonhuman figures.

Any adequate view of the question of stylization will have, moreover, to deal with borderline cases, such as Joseph Sedley in *Vanity Fair* and Alec D'Urberville in *Tess of the D'Urbervilles*. That is, it will have to deal with highly stylized figures that nonetheless strike us as possible, if borderline, representations of "real" people who are dominated by one particular characteristic, such as, in Sedley's case, vanity fused with fatuousness, or in D'Urberville's, melodramatic villainy. Becky Sharp and Tess Durbeyfield teeter on the brink of the same ambiguity, but they lean in the opposite direction. They are in some danger of collapsing out of a convention of relatively mimetic suggestiveness into conventions of literary stereotyping. So, more dramatically, with Shakespeare's Falstaff, Iago, and Enobarbus, among others, who are generated from images of braggart, machiavel, and bluff soldier, respectively.

Other characters, who seem constructed with a view to achieving minimal stylization and thus to simulating "real" presences, are likely—because of the stereotypicality, schematism, and consistency of their behavior—to lapse wholly into types, both life types and literary stereotypes. Mrs. Poyser in *Adam Bede* and Mrs. Cadwallader in *Middlemarch* are such characters.

Coherence

In the classic utterance that I have already cited, Henry James proclaimed, "What is character but the determination of incident? What is incident but the illustration of character?" James's formulation stresses the integral relationship between the characters of a narrative and its plot: how character is revealed in the course of a plot's unfolding. Like most other traditional formulations about character in fiction, it also implies that character exists, to be revealed in the incidents and interactions of a narrative. Like James—and Chatman—I make the same assumption, but I would add that the implicit existence of the creatures (or phantoms, or dream children) who figure in texts as characters must also be assumed to possess greater or lesser degrees of unity, consistency, or coherence. For one of the most striking things about characters in texts is that they need not present themselves as unified or coherent.

The issues of coherence and incoherence, of underlying unity and dissonance, are related to issues already broached in my treatment of stylization. If minimally stylized characters are conceived within the Renaissance and post-Renaissance view of human beings, they—to look ahead to still other terms of my taxonomy—are by definition relatively dynamic, complex figures who are torn by conflict yet are coherent within their underlying identity as established by the text. Maximally stylized figures, on the other hand, may have still another kind of coherence, the coherence of that simplicity or obsessiveness that makes them what they are.

Still, the issues of stylization and coherence, although they overlap, are not identical. Highly coherent characters may be minimally or maximally stylized; the character of Catherine Earnshaw is quite stylized and that of Elizabeth Bennet less so, but both in their different ways strike us as coherent. Similarly, incoherent characters may be either minimally or maximally stylized. Think, for example, of Edmund in *King Lear* in relation to Felix Krull, the Hairy Ape, or the Emperor Jones. All lack coherence, in my sense of the term, but Edmund is less stylized than all the others, Krull is less stylized than the Ape, and the Ape less so than Jones. Hence the need, it seems to me, for a separate scale of qualities concerned with coherence.

At one extreme of the scale of coherence and incoherence we find certain elaborately presented metamorphic or picaresque characters who seem to lack any decisive unifying principle within themselves, except perhaps for the very trait of slipperiness or elusiveness. Such characters tend to be—but need not be—masking characters who deliberately manipulate appearances. Odysseus, in Homer's *Odyssey*, sometimes seem to have this quality, as do his masking, roguelike progeny down through the ages. Shakespeare's Autolychus is one of the more amusing of them; American Indian trickster gods are among the more primitive; Peer Gynt is one of the more complex.

At the other extreme, we find certain radically—even monolithically—consistent, coherent characters whose coherence rests on partializations and fragmentations that preclude any insight into what in life we would call a person's underlying identity. Obviously, strictly allegorical characters fall into this category; so do figures in satire who represent an attitude or a value. Both are by definition wholly of a piece. In the novel, Jaggers in *Great Expectations* is such a figure, as is Tulkinghorn in *Bleak House;* Dickens' lawyers have a tendency to be this kind of character. And Tartuffe, who deforms the law, also belongs to this type. All of these characters are highly stylized in ways that imply the logic of the characters' coherence but do not suggest any particularized psychological ground for it. We do not understand what makes them tick. Such characters are provided with motives, but the motives do not seem adequate within any psychology that might hold for ordinary human beings. Even when they might, we have no meaningful life history to take hold of within which we might place the motive.

Distantly related to such characters are the far less stylized figures of novelistic romance that I discussed briefly in chapter 3. Such figures as Catherine Earnshaw and Heathcliff at first seem more self-evidently coherent than characters of novels such as Elizabeth Bennet, though in the last analysis they are less so. We have a paradox here. The dual protagonists of *Wuthering Heights* are irrevocably split. The split that rends them is the source of the torrential energy that they embody. But the split is so absolute that it epitomizes the one thing that Catherine and Heathcliff are.

Elizabeth Bennet, on the other hand, suffers no such tormenting schism. She is a unified, albeit complex, creature whom we see undergoing a process of self-discovery. Elizabeth experiences conflict and makes choices but never approaches anything like the self-division that afflicts Catherine. Ultimately we are asked to believe that Elizabeth is the one thing that she is, although we are shown nuances of response in her that demand of us a complex synthesis of qualities, of which her coherence is the end product. Her coherence, in this sense, emerges from the synthesis, first by her and then by us, of the whole spectrum of traits that she reveals to us.

The difference beween a Catherine and an Elizabeth, in this respect, lies in the degree of integration of the traits that constitute them. Both strike us as boldly outlined figures that initially convey a sense of coherence. The impression of coherence for each is achieved and asserted in a different way, however, and at a different stage of our process of perception. Catherine *seems* coherent but is in fact fragmented at the root of her being, as she is portrayed in the novel; Elizabeth *is* coherent, in the way that integrated adults in life are. The difference involves elements I shall come to in later sections of this chapter: elements of complexity, of dynamism, of access to inwardness and levels of inwardness. It also relates to aspects of narrative that I shall deal with in the following chapter, aspects having to do with our process of apprehending character.

Catherine and Elizabeth do not figure at opposite ends of the scale that runs from little or no coherence to total, personality-obliterating coherence, yet a considerable range of characters separates them. These characters include those who possess an underlying coherence and unity but whose coherence rests on structures of conflict and contradiction not unlike Catherine's and Heathcliff's, but not nearly so extreme as theirs. The character of Strindberg's Miss Julie has such a structure. She is rent by maddeningly self-contradictory impulses, so much so that she teeters on the brink of the chaos generated by inability to keep her contradictions in balance. Othello is almost as extreme an instance, as are the heroes of much Euripidean, Renaissance, and modern tragedy, all of whom tend to be animated by conflicts of a highly disequilibrating nature. The figures of romantic comedy—Shakespeare's Orsino and Olivia, for example—are strict analogues of such tragic characters: they contain a contradiction that threatens to disrupt the unity of their being but overcome that contradiction through the playing out of the comic plot. Narrative fiction with tragic emphases contains analogous figures. Stendhal's women and Tolstoy's protagonists, like Lawrence's and Woolf's, are such figures.[9] In the postmodernist novel, protagonists tend to polarize into monoliths, on the one hand, and incoherent blobs on the other. Pynchon, in *V.* and Stencil and Benny Profane, dramatizes both possibilities. Bellow's Augie March is similar, with Augie's character amorphous and those of the people he relates to overdefined. Hermann Hesse's crude psychoanalytic novel *Steppenwolf* adumbrates this process, as does the Romantic and post-Romantic tradition of the double.

As with stylization, the concept of coherence involves our cultural biases. When we describe characters as coherent or incoherent, consistent or inconsistent the very terms we use reflect our culture's particular way of conceiving the world. Cultures or epochs that do not show an interest in coherence in character (in whatever sense) generate characters that may not be coherent from our point of view. Ian Watt, for example, holds that Defoe and his readers did not expect unity in characters, and that Moll Flanders, like Robinson Crusoe, reflects a split in values and expectations. He believes that Defoe's contemporaries could hold such contradictions in their minds and not be troubled by them. Hence, for them, Moll could be both a person who exults in her roguish escapades and a penitent.[10] Dorothy Van Ghent takes a very different view of Moll. Like many modern readers, Van Ghent regards Moll as an ironically posed figure whose incoherence helps to make the point of the novel, which concerns the incoherence or the falsity of values in early eighteenth-century England.[11]

One of the curious qualities of such characters as Moll is that they combine incoherence with fullness of detail, or the kind of repletion that we associate with formal realism.[12] Moll, with her discontinuities of attitude and motive, is a richly fleshed-out example. Her presentation makes for the kind of provocative ambiguity that suggests both minimal stylization and great complexity.

Whatever our solution to the problem of coherence in a Moll Flanders or any other character, there is no doubt that within the critical perspectives we tend to share today, the question of coherence is a vital issue. It has in fact been an issue that has vexed critics for centuries and has resulted in the rejection of such characters as Edmund and Othello, and even Iago, because of the difficulty of providing a coherent account of their motives.[13] One reason that postmodernist critics have discounted character as an issue is their refusal to admit the demand for coherence as a standard of value. When Chatman argues for extrapolation of a "paradigm of traits" that "is" a character, he is essentially arguing with the postmodernist school about the value of just this criterion. He is, in effect, seeking grounds acceptable to postmodernist students of poetics for reintroducing a category whose rejection was basic to the postmodernist position.

The postmodernist position would seem to be validated to a considerable extent by the host of characters in literature who refuse coherence and are hard to unify within any single psychological conception of their character, however broad and however dynamic it may be. I have mentioned Edmund's "recantation" as an extreme case of inadequately motivated behavior and have acknowledged Othello and Iago as problems too, at least from the point of view of motivation and consistency. Gertrude and Polonius, in *Hamlet*, present more limited but analogous problems. Gertrude has vexed critics by her uncharacteristically lyrical account of Ophelia's drowning, and some critics have been baffled by the "wisdom" of Polonius' advice to Laertes—advice in which sententiousness, for a moment, falls short of pomposity, and seems to express a wisdom distilled from a lifetime of experience. Actors have dealt with these problems by falling into a declamatory, choral mode for Gertrude and by hamming up the delivery of the speech of Polonius. Both expedients may be necessary, but neither is effective in unifying our conception of these characters.

Such cases are far more difficult to deal with than that of the metamorphic, masking rogue, the protean, picaresque character who takes form and sheds shape as the exigencies of plot and theme require. The discontinuity of such characters as Felix Krull in the modern parodic versions of the rogue tale or of the heroes of the more traditional versions can be taken as a sheer refusal of the criterion of coherence. In its simpler, less sophisticated versions it can also be seen to reflect a lack of consciousness of the demand for the criterion. But Gertrude and Polonius figure in a text that certainly reveals concern with unity of character and motivation. Hence the absence of consistency and coherence becomes a problem and demands attention. The same is true of all of the ruptured and miscarried characterizations, such as those of Maggie Tulliver and Medea, which I mentioned in Chapter 3.

Wholeness

To posit coherence as an aspect of literary characterization is also to invoke some notion of wholeness. A coherent character is likely in one sense to seem a whole character whose substance is made manifest by the various events, interactions, and metaphors of a text. I am concerned here, however, with another aspect of wholeness. We experience wholeness in a character when the character's qualities appear to cohere in such a way as to convince us that what we are given of the character—the segment of his or her putative experience—represents the whole of that character, analogous to the whole of a real person. We feel that the characterization, despite its limitedness, is an exhaustive account of the imagined person that this particular character is meant to be. Forster, we will recall, held that the distinguishing quality of a literary character is the fact that we know all we can know about him or her. In Forster's view, the author knows everything and tells us enough to make us feel that he knows everything and that we know all that we need to know.

There can, of course, be no wholeness in a character in the sense of exhaustiveness or literal comprehensiveness. When we speak of the presentation of character in literature, there is, in fact, no wholeness of prior existence to comprehend. In the end, to be sure, there is no exhaustive wholeness in our conceptualization of people in life either, but for the opposite reason—that there is too much information to be grasped, too much prior existence. Hence any image of a person, in literature or in life, is a selective and interpretative construct, meant to epitomize (or not to epitomize) his or her character or role in some particular situation. From that epitomization one may or may not be able to extrapolate the "Whole" of the person's character. Often we may have much information that yields no gestalt for any sort of wholeness. As I noted in chapter 3, Virginia Woolf held (and Rawdon Wilson echoes her) that repletion is not the ground of characterization. Its proper ground is the pattern of organized and integrated (or integratable) elements that sustain the characterization.[14]

Still, there are ways in which the selected and integrated elements of which the characters are made can be combined to suggest that the phantoms that we construct in our imaginations from words on a page constitute reasonably complete accounts of the particular people we are thinking about. Here "complete account" means, of course, "complete and relevant account," or "complete and relevant evocation." From such an account we may or may not be able to extrapolate in concrete terms more than the elements that immediately engage the reader about them. It seems clear that *Anna Karenina* is designed to give us a whole image of its protagonist, even though there are huge gaps in what we know of her. Although we observe only a segment of such characters' imaginable lives, we feel that we have been given a whole, even an exhaustive, image of them. We have, it seems to me, a similar sense of far less richly elaborated figures, such as Sophocles' Oedipus and Goethe's Faust. Indeed, the sense of a whole image for the latter two is generated in part from what Santayana, writing of Goethe's hero, calls the theme of "ending as completion." Goethe enforces Spinoza's dictum that a life can be contemplated only from the perspective of its ending, of its termination in death.[15]

Finally, the sense of the wholeness of a person in a story or a play rests in part on the extent to which a writer meets the challenge of rendering character coherent from the perspective of the text's ending, which may of course be very different from the character's "ending," or death. In this sense, character creation is always teleological, always serving the needs of the whole imaginative context but itself being generated along the way as an isolable element. Such teleology helps to explain why tragedy, with its emphasis on the ending of the protagonist's life (as well as on the ending of the action in which the hero participates), tends to abound in characters whose wholeness is likely to engage and intrigue us. For tragic writers, death as ending is not the merely conventional way of tying up an action and ending a story, as Forster says it tends to be. Rather, it is the cardinal challenge in the handling of character. What such a writer must do is what Edwin Muir describes in his discussion of novels with a "time" emphasis: the tragic writer must generate a sense of subjective experience of time and in time, which the characters (in the useful phrase that I have earlier borrowed from Keats) must "burn through" to some end, and we with them.[16]

This is why the central figures of so many kinds of works impress us as possessing wholeness. They do so despite the fact that they are caught up in situations that fragment them, often by stirring up conflicts that in fact serve as the occasion for (and center of) the actions in which they figure. Harvey speaks of this quality of protagonists in his discussion of how dimensions of our experience are engaged by the experience of the major characters of fiction. He speaks of the multiplicity of elements in us which are engaged by the multiple dimensions of the characters' being as they struggle with themselves, with others, and with their destinies.[17]

Yet not all works that convey a sense of wholeness engage a complex range of elements within the character. This is what tragedy does, and other genres that depict complex and dynamic characters to whose inwardness we are given a reasonable amount of access; I shall return to such characters in my next chapter. Genres dealing with less complex, less dynamic, and often more highly stylized characters achieve a sense of the wholeness of a character's being in quite other ways.

This is dramatically true of classical (as opposed to romantic) comedy. We feel that we "have" the whole of Volpone or of Molière's Harpagon, despite the extremely limited scope of the motives and conflicts presented. Indeed, the point of *Volpone* and *The Miser* is that the whole of their protagonists' being has been infused into an energizedly obsessive pursuit of their objects. The energy and the sharpness of focus in such works, as well as the elaborate faceting of the action to reveal the dimensions of the protagonists' consuming preoccupations, generate a sense that in the monstrous simplification of aims and motives within them we have the totality of their being. That totality is, implicitly, rooted in their whole life system, and, in terms of some of my other categories, is often largely inaccessible to us owing to the modes of stylization within which they are generated. Such totality belongs to the kind of representation I discussed in my second chapter, where I dealt with the possibility of reading such grotesques as Miss Havisham as examples of arrested development. I shall return to this possibility in the next chapter.

Other kinds of works—works with a strong affinity for comedy—generate a sense of the whole being of a character not by focusing with almost obsessive sharpness on a single person but rather by rendering such a person in the context of highly defined, finely wrought thematic elements. In such works—but also, to a lesser degree, in works that center on a single Volpone- or Harpagon-like character—the sense of the wholeness of a person tends to be a function of the organized thematic structure of the formalized work as a whole, as I noted in my treatment of *Pride and Prejudice* in chapter 3. However narrow the interests of a work and the scale of its engagement with such interests, a firm sense of facets, modes, and levels of response can be generated.

Within the novel, Jane Austen is again an exemplary figure in this respect. Within her "two inches of ivory" and the brittle dance of manners with which she works, the fineness of articulation and engagement creates an Elizabeth whom we *know* and experience not only as charming, intelligent, and interesting but as a being perceived and explored in its wholeness. Such a sense of wholeness is not solely or even chiefly the product of extensive involvement or the large movement of an action but rather a result of the fineness of notation.

An especially interesting aspect of such works as Jane Austen's, which project a sense of the wholeness of their central characters from within the limiting formalization of their comic mode, is the degree of stylization that enters into their projection. Such novels rarely move toward anything approaching maximal stylization in the rendering of their protagonists. Yet they generate a sense of their richly faceted, multidimensional being through the stylization that their artistic mode requires. As we shall see as we move on to the other categories in this chapter, any impulse to equate wholeness, complexity, or dynamism with minimal stylization is fallacious, even though the impulse to make such an equation, stemming as it does from our experience of works of nineteenth-century realism, is easy to understand.

At the other end of the whole–part scale are the characters who are perceived as partial constructs. They may be—they often are—highly coherent and they may even be minimally stylized, but they are on the whole felt to be a function of the action in which they are found and not beings who can be envisioned by themselves in their wholeness. The Fool in *King Lear* is not, by and large, experienced as a whole person whose imagined being can be grasped or significantly elaborated in its own terms. To be understood in any but the most rudimentary motivational sense, he must be resolved back into the dynamic field of emotional, imaginative, and intellectual conflict that animates the play.[18] The same, to a lesser degree, is true of Edgar, as I noted in summing up Janet Adelman's view in chapter 3. It is also true of a multitude of other characters, such as most of Moll Flanders' husbands, or Diggory Venn, the reddleman, in *The Return of the Native*, or Mrs. Elton in *Emma*.

This is probably true, in fact, of most secondary characters in fiction and drama, and it is perhaps the basis for the sharp distinction that Harvey draws between the protagonist who engages us most deeply and the figures who make up the environing world of the work. The secondary figures may, to be sure, have the absoluteness that resides in the fixity their context gives them. They exist, after all, in the "eternity" of organized artifacts. Yet they do not convey a sense of wholeness or dimensionality that ampler presentation, with its teleological thrust and its sharp (if often unresolved) motivational focus, gives to the central figures.[19]

Some secondary figures, it should be noted, manage to upstage the central ones and to take center stage themselves. When this happens, it is not uncommon for the secondary figure to take on the dimensions of wholeness and for the central character not only to remain pallid but also to seem fragmentary. This is what happens, for example, in Dickens' *Our Mutual Friend*, where Bradley Headstone emerges with articulated force and energy as a hauntingly whole character, whose wholeness, like Heathcliff's, resides in the fragmentation of his being. Eugene Wrayburn, for his part, remains a relative stick figure, snarled in the technology of his failed vivification, a character who never generates the illusion of vitality or even of much extension in time and space. A far more dramatic case is to be found in James's *Wings of the Dove*, where Kate Croy materializes as a rich and vivid presence that throws Millie Theale back into the luminous dimness of her insubstantiality. It has been argued that Kate is in fact the central tragic figure of the novel, and this despite James's assertion of Millie's centrality and despite some evidence that she was meant to stand at the center.

In addition to the usurpers of centrality, such as Bradley and Kate, there are the more modest secondary figures who merely transcend their functional roles within the works that generate them. These are the momentary show stealers, such characters as Mercutio and the Nurse in *Romeo and Juliet* and the shepherds in *Oedipus the King*. Some of these characters are related to Harvey's cards: highly energized figures, and often highly stylized, like Mercutio. But they need not be even that. There is, for example, the curious richness that accompanies the figures of nurturing servants, such as Juliet's Nurse, the nurse in *The Libation Bearers*, and Euriclea in the *Odyssey*. Like the protagonists of nineteenth-century fiction or of high tragedy, they come to exist in our consciousness as figures who have a larger existence as integral beings than anything that might be suggested by the scale of their presentation of their function in the text. We cannot say much about them and certainly know virtually nothing about such life experience as they might have had or about the underlying complexities of their hypothetical motives. Yet we do apprehend them as themselves, and as relatively complex beings who tease us with the intimation that we might have done well to know them. Like the Fool and Edgar in *Lear*, and like major characters too, they can be resolved back into the dynamic field of imaginative, emotional, and even intellectual conflict that generates the action of the works in which they figure, but they need not be resolved back into them.

The sense of wholeness of being, stemming somehow from a largeness of presence, in these instances comes, it seems to me, from an amplitude of being conveyed through relatively limited presentational means. With the nurturing figures it may stem from something in us that is addressed by the high artifice of each of the texts involved, something that has to do with tending and nurturing, and our continuing, subterranean preoccupation with nurture. The largeness, wholeness, and amplitude arise in us by virtue of our susceptibility, as elicited by the artifice of the work that calls it forth. Certain images, masterfully placed, and the high concentration of affective stimuli invested in the figure itself are what activate our susceptibility.

There are other kinds of figures that generate a fairly elaborate gestalt, also calling forth intense perceptions and responses in us. With them, however, a vigorous vignettism, such as I noted in my last chapter, is at work, one that operates a high intensity and with highly wrought literary means to generate an illusion of wholeness in the figures involved. Such figures ordinarily appear in relatively short works or in relatively isolated or bracketed fragments of long ones. Within them, an extreme vividness of detail and presentation and an iterative intensity, sustained within a highly compressed structure, generate a keen sense of being—total being, as implied by glimpsed fragments of the whole.

As noted in chapter 3, late medieval literature has a special aptitude for such animation and intensification of the vignette. The Wife of Bath is a great instance of a character who is presented in a limited way—at least as compared with Elizabeth Bennet, Catherine Earnshaw, or Emma Bovary, yet who emerges from the text with a peculiar fullness of being. So, in lesser ways, do the Prioress, the Pardoner, the Knight, and many of the other pilgrims. Dante has a similar gift, exercised with still greater parsimony. Erich Auerbach justly singles out the portrayal of Farinata as a masterpiece of what he calls realism; Farinata has the dimensionality and amplitude that we associate with real people and with characters in effective realistic novels. And so, as Auerbach notes, do a great many of Dante's characters.[20]

Why this is so is not my main concern, but it seems worth

noting that both Dante and Chaucer are writers whose culture was both deeply typological, in the biblical-hermeneutic sense, and radically typifying. Their creations in the realm of characterization tend to be highly intensified versions of familiar social, moral, and literary types—often types who exemplify paradigmatic issues or values. Their peculiar gift in this realm lies in fusing meticulously realistic observation of surface detail with underlying conceptualizations of people and issues. They use the material of observation and experience to qualify the prototypical presuppositions at their disposal, even as they use qualified presuppositions to organize and intensify the material of surface observation. In doing so they suggest not just figures and functions in literature or mere paradigmatic exempla for the moral and spiritual life but whole and complex human beings. They also use the high degree of stylization implicit in their typological modes to create a typifying quality of verisimilitude, such as is often—but not always—implied by the illusion of wholeness in the projection of a person in literature.

Curiously, certain modern writers excel in this too. Gregor Samsa seems to me as vivid an evocation as the Wife of Bath of the wholeness of suggested being. Though we see him only in the constricted nightmare circumstances of Kafka's *Metamorphosis*, the intensity of the experience and its narrative amplification make for a presence so rich that we extrapolate a sense of the whole person. Here too we find an odd combination of a profoundly paradigmatic schematism (including the schematism of the farcical elements that are the literary grid of the story) and almost obsessive concreteness in the notation of subjective response and environmental detail. It seems to me no accident that Kafka achieves this, teetering as he does between a powerful impulse toward allegory and an obsessive (if skeptical) concern with detail, with what he perceived to be the "real" in all its ambiguity and elusiveness.

What I find so interesting in this similarity between Chaucer and Dante on the one hand and Kafka on the other is the fact that writers with deep traditions of allegorical typification or strong impulses toward typifying reduction do so well at intimating the complexity of whole being, combining their typological propensities with a countervailing preoccupation with particularizing detail. This, to my mind, confirms the typological principle put forward in my second chapter and adds further dimension to it. Earlier, I held that we perceive typologically, moving from perception of the more general to perception of the more particular. If it is true that the great vignettists who generate partial images that suggest wholeness are great typologists, then it would seem that the generation of character rests in large part on prior typifications. The implication is that in literature as in science, figures and other patterns are not generated by direct observation and combination of particulars—that is, that they are formed not inductively and inferentially, but rather by deduction from prototypes and patterns.

One further sign of this typifying propensity is a more radical aspect of the whole–part phenomenon, the entire range of synecdochic and metonymic strategies for generating characters. These strategies are often employed in very highly stylized characterizations, although they figure in all processes of character projection. Forster's definition of flat characters as one-trait constructs seems relevant here. Forster stressed the Dickensian trick of using tag phrases, noting the relationship of such strategies to caricature. What is implied by the one-trait and tag phrase system is a kind of synecdochic reduction of an imaginary person, whose wholeness, as made possible by being named or designated, can be apprehended by means of the limiting trait or phrase, the mode of its iteration, and the context of its manifestation. In Dickens' novels, a character is often summed up— epitomized, as it were—in a synecdochic image or series of images. Thus Jaggers, as perceived by Pip, virtually becomes his finger. Similarly, the hero of Gogol's "Nose" becomes a nose, and Akaky Akakievich, in *The Overcoat*, is closely identified first with his shoes and then with his overcoat. In each case, the organ, trait, or appurtenance is woven into a thematic system that confers meaning upon it and feeds back into our sense of the character. Hence the threateningness of Jaggers' finger becomes the punitiveness of the law, and the obsessive laving of the hand to which it is attached becomes the guilt—including Jaggers' guilt—that sustains the law. Both threat and guilt are siphoned into the humanly opaque Jaggers to suggest the substance that informs him as a "whole" being—as the thing that, in his curtailed way, he is.

In more complex, multiple-trait characters, the process of elaboration and epitomization is more complex but not very different. The essential Casaubon, in *Middlemarch*, is identified with the labyrinths, catacombs, and cloaca of his mind, and finally of his bowels. The images are then elaborated through the system of selfishness within which he manifests himself. Casaubon is not merely his angry, anal self, but his complex self is constantly referred back to these metaphors (labyrinths, catacombs, cloaca), which, by identification with his guts, become synecdoches. In analogous ways, a large variety of characters are identified with their houses, as in *Wuthering Heights*. For a moment, at the end of her life, as Roman Jakobson notes, Anna Karenina is identified with her handbag, even as the little princess whom Prince Andrei marries in *War and Peace* is identified with her short upper lip.[21]

Clearly, as even my limited examples should show, the more complex identifications and sometimes the simpler ones as well use their synecdoches and metonymies for thematic and structural purposes. Indeed, synecdoche and metonymy are two of the numerous means of integrating characters within the total literary structure of a work, as with the network of images related to houses in *The Portrait of a Lady*, where the imagery serves as a vehicle for both character elaboration and thematic integration. At the same time that they function in thematic terms, such images also generate a sense of the character's personality and moral being. The house imagery in *Wuthering Heights* is a classic example, working vividly to help us understand what animates Catherine and Heathcliff in their rage to merge. And then, of course, we have Captain Ahab's whale-ivory peg leg.

Whatever psychological frame of reference we chose, such use of a part of a person's whole being or of some element in the context of the person's being to convey a sense of the person or to provide an explanation of his or her motives has deep roots in the conceptualization of people in our intellectual and literary traditions. In the old system of humors, for example, character was conceived of in terms of the dominance of a single humor, or disposition. In other systems (such as Aristotle's) character was thought of as being organized around a dominant trait. Even the dynamic contemporary psychology of the unconscious assumes that certain dominant modes of conflict and conflict resolution color and define the individual. Stanislavsky, in advising a young actor how to prepare to act a character, stressed the value of isolating some characteristic gesture or other feature of expression as the basis for projecting that character in performance.

Still, despite the universality of this metaphoric way of presenting character, the extent, mode, and resonance of its use vary widely. As with my first two categories—I mean stylization/schematization and coherence—the metonymic strategy for wholeness must be conceived on a curve that permits the largest range of possibilities: from such characters as Casaubon and Anna Karenina, in whom it is difficult (though always possible) to isolate the part or moment that represents the whole, to those like Jaggers, in whom the part is the whole. Jakobson to the contrary, Anna Karenina as a whole cannot essentially be identified with her handbag; she is identified with it only at a particular moment. We follow her in this association within a carefully defined context whose significance and intensity rest in part on that flicker of identification. Indeed. Jakobson's equation of realism in character portrayal with metonymy seems to me fallacious, except in the sense that nineteenth-century realism depends on close reciprocity between characters and the things that are contiguous with them. Within the tradition of realism, these things, taken all together, constitute the social and historical environment in which the characters are presented. Other kinds of metonymy, however, are possible within modes of minimal stylization that precede and follow the epoch of nineteenth-century realism. Thus in Shakespeare or Racine the metonymies are more fluid and sequential and reflect the dynamism of conflict and development. They operate at a tangent to the social and historical context but in relation to people and to psychic or cosmic forces. On the other hand, the synecdochic element in Jaggers' characterization is rather rigid and fixed, permitting the summation of his being in a gesture or a set of gestures that are essentially isolated from a historical environment and relate instead to the thematic structure of issues having to do with guilt, accusation, judgment, manipulation, and appropriation of others.

To speak of synecdoche and metonymy, I should note, is in one respect to cloud my field of discourse. I am arguing that certain characterizations suggest the wholeness of a person, whereas others constitute glimpses of a possible person. For the latter, I hold, we may if we choose postulate a range of experience and even a life history. Generally, speaking, however, texts that generate fragmentary or incomplete characters do not ask us to do that, and we instinctively and automatically refrain from trying. The impression we take is so fleeting and partial that we are not impelled to consider the figure as a whole being. Now, to invoke a figure of speech that gives us the part for the whole—"sail" for ship or "hands" for workers— is to imply that every character constitutes some sort of "whole." Clearly, the question is a semantic one. In speaking of synecdoches and metonymies, I mean to suggest that the portion of a character's person or experience or context that is expressed in the metaphor helps to generate a sense of the whole of that person *as he or she is in the text*. Whether the "whole," such as it is, further suggests a whole person on the analogy of a whole person in life is a further question with which the bulk of this section, on parts and wholes, has been concerned.

It seems to me that the process of epitomizing characters through such classical rhetorical devices as synecdoche is one of the primary ways of generating all characters—minimally as well as maximally stylized ones, complex as well as simple ones. My examples, which polarize a Jaggers and a Casaubon, are designed to suggest this. Synecdochic epitomization is central in generating partial characters as well as whole ones. The reason for this, I would hold, is the essentially typifying ground of our conception of character, which we have looked at in connection with Chaucer, Dante, and Kafka in this section and also in my second chapter. Only in texts that deny the possibility of generalizing or epitomizing the nature of the characters—as in many postmodernist novels—does this principle fail to work.

Literalness

Just as characters can be ranged on a scale of greater or lesser stylization, greater or lesser coherence, and greater or lesser wholeness, so they can be said to partake of a greater or lesser degree of literalness in their presentation and in their place within the total configuration of meaning within a work.

As with wholeness, literalness is a highly relative and entirely unobtainable quality. Since all of the elements in literature are symbolic, no single element refers to anything "literally," except as a sort of bracketed quotation. By this I mean that even the use of New York or Moscow as the setting of a story, or the use of Napoleon or Herakles as an agent in a poem or story, refers primarily not to place, person, or mythical figure in and for itself but to some conceptualization of it within a structure of meanings that is essentially metaphoric. Postmodernist criticism refers to this phenomenon when it holds that literature in general contains signifiers that signify nothing in the world outside, the "world out there." And it is certainly true that characters in literature commonly refer to no literally existent being.

Historical figures in novels or plays, such as Napoleon and Kutuzov in *War and Peace* or Richard in *Richard II*, do not refer significantly or literally to the people by those names who once existed in the world. Rather, like any other character, they elicit a range of organized perceptions of a fictive person—in this case a person who represents the author's conception of someone who has existed in history. Even if the emphasis on the historicity of the image is considerable, as in *War and Peace*, the image is necessarily an image within the total literary structure, which can refer meaningfully to the world outside itself only in terms of the work's whole configuration of meaning, and only as a metaphoric totality at that.[22] Tolstoy's Napoleon is modeled on a conception of the historical Napoleon and on a reading of the place of such a figure as Napoleon—that is, of the "literally" historical Napoleon. We need knowledge of the historical Napoleon to understand Tolstoy's work, but in reading the novel we can use such knowledge only in Tolstoy's terms.

Figures not directly presented as historical are, if possible, a still simpler matter. Whatever the disingenuousness of declarations that "the characters in this novel bear no resemblance to any person living or dead," in fact characters in literature, even when ostensibly "based" on real-life "models," are constructs based on the writers' readings of the models—constructs that, however verisimilar, bear little significant relation to their models. Their significant relation is to the configuration of links to other elements within the structure of the works in which they appear. As "copies" of "real" people they have the same status as all the other "unreal," imagined, fabricated figures in the work. This is true even, or especially, in the work of such writers as D. H. Lawrence, who is notorious for "putting" real people in his novels. That Miriam in *Sons and Lovers* "is" Jessie Chambers or that Gudrun and Gerald in *Women in Love* "are" Katherine Mansfield and Middleton Murry is a historical curiosity and may offer some insight into Lawrence's creative (and destructive) process. But it can tell us little that matters about the issues of the novels in which they appear and cannot illuminate the characters "based" on them. Gudrun is herself and also figures symbolically within the play of tensions that makes up the pattern of *Women in Love*. She is, in my manner of speaking here, at once "literally" herself and, as herself, can also symbolize a certain kind of woman within a pattern of sexual, psychological, moral, and historical issues.

It is in this sense that one can speak of the literalness of characters and of a scale of literalness, as well as of symbolic or extraliteral thrust in several directions. Characters can be taken to be more or less literal and more or less symbolic: of themselves, of qualities they embody, and of human types and possibilities. That is, characters can be spoken of as literally themselves—as signifying the particular thing that each of them is—or as signifying something else, such as qualities they themselves embody, human types they exemplify, or ideas they represent.

The distinction may be simplistically exemplified by the contrast between Oedipus and Everyman. Oedipus can easily be taken to represent (or epitomize) dilemmas and responses so universally human that he is readily transformed into a paradigm of Man—into a kind of Everyman. Yet however paradigmatic his situation and however relevant his pattern of responses and his motivational system may be to all of us, Oedipus in Sophocles' *Oedipus the King* remains irrevocably himself. He remains a being (albeit a fictional one) who is felt to undergo an experience that is uniquely and agonizingly his own and that can only secondarily be seen or generalized as an exemplum.[23] Everyman, on the other hand, has no particularized experience that we can take to be his own. He is all paradigm, all exemplum.

The polarity between allegorical figure and tragic hero exemplifies my terms. Most characters in literature may be located between the two poles, embracing a considerable range of possibilities. Among characters who are essentially coherent, Anna Karenina, Emma Bovary, and Regan in *King Lear* provide convenient examples of gradations on the scale.

Anna Karenina, once we have perceived the global configuration of her being, is apprehended primarily as herself—the particular, named woman, Anna Karenina—and secondarily as an adulteress, an inadequate mother, or a narcissist crumbling into incoherence. And even insofar as she is this series of generalized things, it is hard to make a single pattern of them except within the moralized thesis of the novel, which ambivalently must damn her for her moral deviation. Tolstoy fails to transpose his marvelous heroine into the epitome of adultery, of whom we can believe that "vengeance is mine, saith the Lord." Her actions may come to seem paradigmatic, but she herself does not quite lend herself to the paradigm. Tolstoy, as sensitive readers of the novel have noted, loved her far too much.

Emma Bovary, for her part, although we have been told that she was Flaubert (or rather that Flaubert was she), is dramatically herself, but nonetheless she is, more than Anna, a certain kind of woman, a certain kind of person, one who loses herself in fantasy, who milks her feelings to generate a tenuous, fleeting sense of self, who finally destroys herself by doing so. Regan, in turn, although she is a commanding presence, is barely seen as herself. She is perceived largely as a wicked daughter, deceitful sister, conniving wife—as a human incarnation of bestiality, along the lines of the epithets used to characterize her in the course of the play. Yet she still has more self-reference and particularity than Everyman.

Within a single work, different characters can serve to denote different degrees of self-reference or reference to something beyond themselves. In *Bleak House*, for example, Lady Dedlock is fabricated out of a set of generalized qualities and stereotypes; she is Idol of the Fashionable Intelligence; black-clad, threatening, witchlike, Morgan-le-Fay; wicked stepmother; faithless lover; damned adulteress. Yet by the end of the action we have the sense that she is "inhabited" by her own repressed but warm, even melting, feelings, and that she is, if we believe the novel, incorrigibly herself. As such she then suggests the tragedy of lost love and all its anguish. Hortense, her maid, on the other hand, although Dickens works overtime in various scenes to localize her passion as her own, is never felt to contain or to sustain her own experience as a person to whom we might give even momentary credence. She remains the distillation of manipulative vindictiveness, the stereotype of the jealous lady's maid, and of a threateningly foreign one at that. The information we get about her explains her passion, but the novel gives us no way of apprehending it as being her own.

More extreme in their lack of self-reference to themselves as simulacra of people are the almost purely functional characters in Dickens. In *Bleak House*, Guppy is, in his way, such a character—someone we can detach from the action and contemplate but who is basically there to perform a function in the action. Silbermann, in Nabokov's *Real Life of Sebastian Knight* (already referred to in chapter 3), is a more extreme instance of such functionality. He is neither given to be contemplated as himself nor is essentially symbolic of anything beyond himself, unless we think of him as symbolic of the text, as the composite of its components. Gower, in Shakespeare's *Pericles*, is such a figure, as are the heterodiegetic narrators of many tales, who may serve as nothing but the medium for conveying a story and as a cipher in the text code that dramatizes itself.

Obviously, both self-referential and symbolic characters exist in the same work; it is inconceivable that any work of literature should contain only characters who represent themselves. Less obvious, but not infrequent, is the possibility of both qualities inhering in a single character, usually a character who is somewhat incoherent too. Leontes, in *A Winter's Tale*, it seems to me, is one of them, figuring at the beginning of the play largely as a paradigmatic example of a jealous husband and at the end as a jealous husband who digests his own experience. The opposite sequence is to be seen in Orsino, in *Twelfth Night*. The Orsino of the opening is sufficiently engrossed in his romantic fantasies to pass as a being whose particularized inwardness is expressed by the poetry of his excess, whereas the Orsino of the conclusion is the stick figure of comic resolutions.

On the whole, it seems to me that Shakespeare's romances and his comedies, especially his problem comedies, abound in such figures, as do the histories. It may be that madly mixed genres tend to generate such hybrids, with the characters accommodating to the shifting demands of the composite generic structure but not arriving at the point of suggestive synthesis that, as I noted in chapter 3, Moll and Shylock achieve in *Moll Flanders* and *The Merchant of Venice*. The same, in principle, may be the case with, say Coriolanus or Timon of Athens, whose standing within the anomalous tragic structures they inhabit could be explained on such a principle. So, indeed, would all the difficult-to-factor characters in Jacobean tragedy, where, as traditional criticism has it, character is shifted or faceted to meet the needs of individual scenes, as with De Flores in *The Changeling* or with Vindice in *The Revenger's Tragedy,* or even with Antonio and Victoria in *The Duchess of Malfi* and *The White Devil*

As my examples should suggest, this category—literalness—intersects at many points with other categories already treated—coherence and wholeness for example. A radical lack of coherence marks a character whose reactions seem arbitrary, as those of Leontes, Pericles, and Antonio often do. It is difficult to develop a sense of unity, wholeness, or motivational logic within such systematic but unexplained shifts, even when modulation from one mode to another is carefully managed. In principle, moreover, the pair of terms used here—*literal* and *symbolic*—coincides in part at least with another pair of terms commonly used in discussing character. I mean *individual* and *type*. Characters who are given as literally themselves are more likely to be perceived as individuals than characters who are given as representatives of a class.

Again, Oedipus is, to begin with, primarily Oedipus—"himself alone," as I have put it—while Everyman is from beginning to end the very pattern of all men. Oedipus, insofar as he is literally himself and not symbolic of any other, may or may not be regarded as an individual, individuality being a characteristic that clearly did not engross Sophocles as it did Hegel or the brothers Schlegel. Whether or not we take him to be an individual, however, he is clearly meant to be thought of as himself. Literalness, in this sense, is a broader category than individuality, though one that does not subsume it exhaustively.

The relationship between individuality and literalness which I am suggesting is complicated but is reinforced, it seems to me, by two central facts. First, as I noted in the preceding section, certain typological preconceptions, such as Chaucer's and Dante's, are conducive to the production of highly individualized characters, such as Farinata and the Wife of Bath, whom we tend to grasp as literally themselves. In Chaucer, even the most typified figures, such as the characters in the beast fables, are likely to flip into their opposites—into such individuated figures as Chauntecleer and Pertelote. Second, even characters who chrystallize in our consciousness as highly individualized often flip into figures that epitomize whole classes of people. We need only to think of Don Quixote and the quixotic, or of Hamlet and all our hamletizings. Don Quixote and Hamlet are very much themselves, and in a way are exclusively themselves. So much is this the case that the essential pattern of qualities that makes them what they are is easily generalized, or adjectivized. The reason for this phenomenon is, of course, double. It reflects the typifying ground of all our perceptions, and not only our perceptions of people, as I noted in chapter 2. And it stems from the fact that any individual with certain qualities vividly intensified becomes representative of the type he or she embodies.

Our assumption of a sharp polarity between individual and type is highly misleading. Hence the importance of perceiving the process, in character creation, of movement from one pole to the other and of apprehending the process whereby what I have been calling the literal reference of character to that quality which is itself can generate a symbolic representation of something generalized and other than itself and of the process whereby the generic, the typical, and the symbolic can generate images of people whom we take to be literally themselves.

Complexity

Closely related to and often intersecting the literal–symbolic axis is the distinction between simple and complex characters. The distinction plays a part within Jane Austen's *Pride and Prejudice*, where Elizabeth tells Darcy that people can be divided into the simple and the complex.[24] Elizabeth, in fact, is complex, and so is Darcy; Jane Bennet, like Bingley, is simple. Jane Austen's novels are wonderfully illustrative of the distinction, probably in large part because of the carefully calibrated scale on which they are constructed. As in most novels, Austen's central figures are usually more or less complex, while the flanking characters seem more or less simple, or at least more stylized. To this extent, the distinction between the two types is largely that, defined by Harvey, of central as opposed to secondary characters. A Jane Bennet is chiefly herself: she is not a symbolic, easily generalized type figure. But she is a simple "literal" figure, unmarked by the complex cross-currents of ambivalence that characterize Elizabeth.

Yet the simple correlation breaks down if we examine flanking characters more stylized than Jane, such characters as Mrs. Bennet in *Pride and Prejudice* and Mr. Woodhouse in *Emma*. Once we do so, it becomes clear that there is no simple, schematic scale of declining complexity as we move from the center to the periphery of a complex work. Mrs. Bennet, viewed closely, is a very complex creature indeed, if not, in the manner of her presentation, a highly developed or conscious one. The relatively simple, schematic, caricaturistic mode of her presentation does not imply simplicity of motive or of psychic structure. If anything, it implies an exceedingly devious and complex system of evasions and circumventions within a radically unselfconscious mentality. The same is true of Mr. Woodhouse. Both of them are shown to possess a highly infantile narcissism. Mrs. Bennet's works through lethal identification with her daughters' sexuality, as expressed in her close identification with Lydia; Mr. Woodhouse's through a denial of his own appetites and a need to suppress everyone else's, as expressed at one point in his attempt to withhold chicken with oyster sauce from his guests.

Chatman's static construct, the paradigm of traits, is inadequate to describe this kind of complexity. What makes Mrs. Bennet more complex than Jane and even in her way than Elizabeth is not the fact that she is compounded of more traits. It is the fact that her traits implicitly form a dynamic system of stresses that suggest greater complexity—that is, a high degree of inner tension and self-contradiction in enacting herself. Such complexity is related to the blindness and evasiveness of the "heavies" of traditional comedy—the "blocking figures," often grotesque, that Northrop Frye describes in his account of New Comedy.[25]

The kind of simplicity that Elizabeth is talking about—the kind that Jane Bennet exemplifies, and that Jane Austen manages so artfully—is usually to be found in works employing some degree of limited, if not necessarily minimal, stylization. That simplicity tends to overlap with the simplicity of innocents and fools, which I discussed in relation to stylization. Highly stylized works also tend to produce another kind of simplification, which I discussed as a kind of "wholeness—a simplicity that dramatically substitutes a single part for the whole of the person, endowing characters with one trait, or a very limited number of traits, and dealing with those traits grotesquely.

The examples of Mrs. Bennet and Mr. Woodhouse, however, suggest a further complicating factor. They are the most grotesque figures—on the whole, highly stylized ones—in works whose other characters tend to be far less stylized. The blocking "heavies" of traditional comedy, to which I referred in the last paragraph, are further extremes of such characterization. They are figures that are mocked for their seeming simplicity and for their rigidity and grotesqueness, but they often prove to have very complex motivations indeed. Mr. Osborne, in *Vanity Fair*, is such a figure. He proves less simple and grotesque than he first seems, and he betrays an all-too-human vulnerability. At that point, as happens with Miss Bates in *Emma*, the degree of stylization lessens, and the character lapses into another mode, which proves to be less complex than the previous stylized mode. The same is true of the rendering of Miss Havisham, in whom considerable complexity of motivation is suggested within the highly stylized but reductive rendering of her static state throughout her first appearances. Yet when she breaks out of her constraining compulsions and reaches out for the humanity of contact with Pip by asking his forgiveness, the mode—or perhaps only the degree—of stylization changes, and much of the complexity bleeds out of the presentation.

When this happens, the categories of coherence and wholeness, together with degrees and modes of stylization, come into play, in our apprehension of these characters. The modulation from complexity to simplicity and simplicity to complexity in fact implicates the whole range of categories we have brought to bear on characters so far. This modulation figures as a separate category, however, because of the seemingly odd combinations that may develop play with regard to specific characters: complexity joined with maximal stylization and simplicity combined with lesser stylization; wholeness joined with simplicity and partiality accompanied by complexity.

Transparency

Characters are not only simpler or more complex; they are also more or less open to us, allowing us greater or lesser access to direct perception of their inwardness. Thus, to take the characters in *Pride and Prejudice* again, Jane is simple, and her motives, after having been withheld for a while, become utterly transparent. Mrs. Bennet, on the other hand, is complex, and her motives are for the most part (and on the face of it, at least) largely opaque. What is true of Mrs. Bennet is also true of Mr. Woodhouse. We can "read" him, and read him richly, but only in terms of a contextual and behavioral code that is inaccessible to him, to most of those who surround him in the novel, and to the naive or unreflecting reader.

The degree to which characters are accessible to themselves and to us can, like all of the other aspects of character, vary widely within the same work and even within the same character at different moments of experience. In *Great Expectations*, Jaggers' motives are less visible than Miss Havisham's, Miss Havisham's than Wemmick's, and Wemmick's than Pip's. It is on the whole true that highly stylized, rigidly schematicized grotesques tend to be less transparent as to motive than minimally stylized, relatively realistic ones. Yet minimal stylization is no guarantee of accessibility as to motive and character structure, nor, in fact, does the use of such techniques as soliloquy and stream of consciousness, which seem to open people's minds to us, ensure access. Thus, for example, Patrick White, in *The Living and the Dead*, employs a highly stylized technique involving much free, indirect discourse, kaleidoscopic imagery, and time distortion to render the experience of the characters. But the characters' motives are deliberately allowed to remain obscure. The same is true of many of the characterizations in Proust, where there sometimes seems to be an inverse relationship between the amount of consciousness and sensibility that is unfurled for a character and the extent to which we penetrate the more inward layers of the character's personality and motivations. Shakespeare's heroes—Prince Hal, for example, especially in his first soliloquy—often disclose motives that make it difficult for us to piece out a coherent sense of who they are meant to be and how we are to understand them.

Within a single work there can, moreover, be striking shifts in the degree to which inwardness is accessible. In *Great*

Expectations, as Miss Havisham moves toward the end of her trajectory, we are increasingly invited to perceive and to participate in her emotions. She is, as I noted in the section on simple and complex characters, progressively "humanized" for us as she becomes more and more accessible to Pip, whose adult memory of her is ostensibly the medium through which we become aware of her. This does not, again, mean that she becomes more effective as a character; she in fact seems to me to become a less effective one, because she becomes a less consistent and a less energized one. Her effectiveness within the novel rests to a considerable extent on the opacity of the highly charged fantasticality of her existence for Pip. Similarly, Pip becomes both more transparent and less interesting as the novel moves toward its close. His renunciation of his expectations, and with it of his obscure but brilliant fantasy life, makes him a less suggestive figure, if a more graspable and, in the novel's official view, more admirable one.

Such shifts in openness also affect the coherence and the wholeness of characters. Since it is difficult to track Pip's development, the transparency of the latter parts of the novel ruptures our sense of the coherence, however obscure, that characterized him before. With Miss Havisham, the augmented openness of her presentation affects not only coherence but our sense of her wholeness. The entire development makes sense, but the discrepant modes and the problematic modulations make it hard for us to keep the whole of her in consciousness.

An engaging opacity is often a characteristic of the heroes of some of Shakespeare's comedies. We don't and can't know why Olivia withdraws from life in mourning for her brother. An obscure "incestuous" motive may be posited, and when we consider it, especially in the context of the curious sexual patterns at work in virtually all of the major characters in *Twelfth Night*, we are led to feel that there is something threatening and even perverse in her sexuality. But we cannot know this with any certainty with reference to Olivia herself as a particular person. Her liberation from her obsession—a release secured by the workings of the plot as a kind of providence—makes for a great clarity of motivation and a considerable reduction of our sense of her being, but it provides us with little retrospective clarity as to the springs of her behavior.

Accessibility would seem to have something to do with degrees of stylization and with the extent to which characters are designed to seem literal or symbolic. Insofar as characters are drawn in minimally stylized ways, with open dramatization of their consciousness as they digest their experience, we would seem to have direct access to their motives and to be assured of a clear sense of who and what they are, at least with regard to motives. It might also seem fairly self-evident that insofar as characters are maximally stylized, we might be prevented from seeing into their consciousness and therefore be consistently confronted with blanks with regard to motives.

Yet the opposite would often seem to be the case. When we are given direct access to the motives of minimally stylized, relatively realistic characters, we often come to realize that we cannot exhaust their motives, just as we often cannot fathom the motives of people in life. More than that. Sometimes clear motives are given, motives that are sufficient for the needs of the plot—of its "realistic motivation"—and of our superficial response to the plot. Yet the designated motives prove inadequate to our understanding of the character. Gilbert Osmond, in *The Portrait of a Lady*, is a case in point. We know exactly why he marries Isabel: for her money. He is, at a certain level, the prototype of the villains in marriage-market melodrama. But that motive does not suffice for *The Portrait of a Lady* as it is written. First of all, he is too authentically charming to be merely a fortune hunter. As Dorothea Krook insists, Isabel is too intelligent, too charming, too vividly alive to fall in love with the arrant manipulator he would have to be at that level.[26] However greedy and manipulative he may be, he must, it turns out, be in love and capable of being in love in order for the plot to work. But beyond that, he must also be animated by a whole network of further motives if we are to account for the moral sadism of his relationship to all the women he is involved with; that is, to Isabel, to Pansy, to Madame Merle, and to his sister. To that level of motivation, however, we have no direct access. All we have is a set of images—romance images, and diabolical ones—to underscore both his function within the novel and the issues that might be relevant in our understanding of him.

James, to be sure, is renowned for his handling of ambiguity, and if ambiguity is operative at all other literary levels it should be operative at the level of character as well. Yet it is not in James alone that motives lend themselves to ambiguous readings. Many interesting motivational systems tend to lead us into motivational dead ends, since literature need not (and often cannot) lead us to the very bottom of any kind of behavior. This is, again, one of the points of congruity between literature and life, but also of difference. In life, with a possibility of a full life record (including a budget of "free" associations), we may be able to reach a viable hypothesis about the grounds of behavior. In literature, though the basic pattern may emerge with clarity, there is no way of reaching any degree of certainty as to particulars in the presumed background of experience of a character.

Opacity, or rather partial opacity, may seem to blend into incoherence. In principle, I would hold that it doesn't, even though in practice it may on occasion do so. The difference is between unresolvedness and contradiction, between an impression of unity in the conception of a character and the impression of underlying disunity. The difference can be exemplified by the contrast between those of Shakespeare's comic heroes whose characterological complexion changes in the movement toward resolution of the plot, without any grounds within the previous action, and those of James's heroes who merely remain unfactorable. It is the difference, say, between Bertram, in *All's Well That Ends Well*, and

Osmond in *The Portrait of a Lady*. The emphasis in Bertram is on mere movement or change; in Osmond, the emphasis in on the unity of his being, which is felt to comprehend all of the possible facets of need and desire within him. Osmond is clearly a masker and a manipulator, but James suggests, and his generic indicators insist, that Osmond is one thing, one complex being, like the rest of us. So much is this so that James can be seen to strive to avoid even the appearance of contradictions in point of motives; *The Portrait of a Lady* facilitates our factoring of motives as part of the tissue of complexities that life is seen to be. Part of that complexity, again, is the difficulty of rationally extrapolating a whole, coherent pattern of impulses and motives.

This difficulty may be the ground of the greatest characterizations in literature. Meir Sternberg notes that in Shakespearean tragedy we never adequately know why the hero does what he does.[27] How true this finally is does not concern me here; that it is true up to a point is clear. Also true is the fact that the dramatistic structure of Shakespeare's plays contributes to the opacity of the characters at certain points, an opacity that works for the better or the worse depending on the context. In play after play, Shakespeare frames his actions in terms of plots within plots, with one character placing another within a fictive situation and reacting to hypothetical challenges as though they were real. This is what happens when Polonius stages Hamlet's encounter with Ophelia and when Iago stages the bedroom exchange with Cassio and the handkerchief exchange between Cassio and Bianca to provoke Othello's response. In each case the creation of a new theatrical or dramatistic frame elicits a new response that generally leaves more than usually large gaps in motivation. Such gaps, which are often permanent, make for opacity. And just this failure to know with clarity the "whys" of action and choice is one of the grounds of the verisimilitude that marks the tragedies, a ground that operates together with richly suggestive constellations of motives to sustain and justify the final obscurity.[28] Such constellations are not murky; each of them tends to be embedded in a pattern of elements that sustain and explicate it. The various motives, as I have noted about Moll Flanders in my section on coherence, tend to make a pattern, though an ambiguous one.

On the other hand, and sharply opposed to the tragic hero in Shakespeare, there are characters whose motives we absolutely do not know, and need not know, as well as characters whose motivation is as clear and simple as their actions. The latter's number is legion. Todorov's narrative men are of this sort. We know what they are so that we may know what they will do. But knowing who or what they are is synonymous with knowing their motives, and hence they are utterly transparent. As for those whose motives we do not know, they too abound. Why is Mr. Skimpole irresponsible? He just is, because he wishes to be as carefree as a bird or a child. But why? There is no reliable verifiable answer, except such as can be obtained from within the thematic concerns of *Bleak House*. Part of the pleasure of responding to character as such lies in the degrees of opacity with which characters' motives are presented to us and in the almost teasing quality of the limits put on our capacity to puzzle out those motives. The art of literature altogether lies in directing lines of vision in such a way as to engage us with certain aspects of a "subject," theme, or form and to deflect our consciousness from other aspects. This is what James meant when he said that the house of fiction has many windows and that the art of composition lies in choosing which windows to see through. Literature gives us eyes to see with as well as apertures to see through and into, more or less clearly, more or less deeply.

It would be a piece of rank obscurantism to conclude my treatment of transparency (as opposed to opacity) in character with the statement that, paradoxically, obscurity is the end product of even the greatest openness.[29] What must be noted, in conclusion, is that characters do present themselves to our consciousness in terms of greater and lesser transparency as to motives and that such transparency is not chiefly a

matter of exposed consciousness. This aspect of their presentation must be weighed, together with the other elements I
have enumerated—that is, together with degrees of stylization,
measure of coherence, extent of wholeness, literalness, and
complexity, as well as with the qualities of dynamism and
closure that I discuss in the sections that follow.

Dynamism

Dynamic characters and their opposites, static ones, figure
in my next polarity. From within my self-declared perspective,
which defines conflict and the dynamism that it generates as
the ground of character, static characters should not exist. Yet
within the surface structure of texts (and it is with surface
structure that we are concerned here), not all characters are
presented, and hence not all characters are perceived, as
dynamic. Even if we wish to interpret all characters in terms
of their implicit dynamism, we must first acknowledge that
works of literature, past and present, contain manifestly
static as well as dynamic characters, and that whatever
implicit dynamism we may wish to attribute to the static
ones, their dynamism issues in static surfaces: the surfaces
presented in the text.

We all know more or less what we mean by dynamic
characters. They are, on the whole, relatively complex characters who develop, or "change." They are the equivalent of
Forster's "round" characters, creatures who undergo crises of
experience and who shift and adapt in response to them. In
chapter 3 I offered Elizabeth Bennet as a limited model for
such characters. Emma Woodhouse provides a richer instance.
Shakespeare's tragic heroes belong to this group; so do the
heroes of most other tragedies; so do the heroes of the great
nineteenth-century realistic novels and the heroes of the
Bildungsroman in its various kinds. Certain early twentieth-
century works—*A Portrait of the Artist as a Young Man, Sons
and Lovers*, and *Remembrance of Things Past* are extreme and
striking examples—fuse qualities of the realistic novel and

the *Bildungs-cum-Kunstlerroman*. Such works generate characters and structures that not only suggest the wholeness of the protagonist and of his life experience but suggest it while dramatizing the dynamic processes of the conscious and unconscious life. Such works tend to be minimally stylized in presentation of central character and consciousness; tend to dramatize an elusive but pervasive coherence in the character's response to experience; tend to be extremely literal in their insistence that the character at the center refers to himself alone and only afterward may be taken as the prototype of whatever he is; and often give us vivid access to the obscurest of motives.

At the opposite pole are the fixed, the static characters of farce, melodrama, and certain kinds of romance. The figures of primitive commedia dell'arte belong to this group; so do many of the highly stylized characters of ballad and fairy tale. Indeed, the Theophrastan character, which is the ancestor of all stock or comic characters in the European tradition, belongs to this class. The Theophrastan character cannot change because it is not implicated in meaningful narrative—that is, temporal—sequences. Frye is speaking of this kind of character when he describes stock figures as the ground on which all individualized characters are developed. Such characters tend to be highly fragmentary, though they are often highly coherent, significantly symbolic, and transparent in motive.

As with my other polarities, there are many in-between stages. Certain of Jane Austen's minor, seemingly static characters have been discussed, since Forster at least, as potentially developing figures. Forster brings Lady Bertram, with her sudden, unlikely awakening into moral consciousness, as an example. Miss Bates, with her flash of unexpected vulnerability to Emma's insult at Box Hill, is a still better example.

Characters who can convincingly surprise us by manifesting a hitherto concealed trait have been central to lectures on fiction by H. M. Daleski. Daleski holds that Forster's polari-

ty of flat and round characters does not take into account
characters who, like Lady Bertram or, still more, Miss Bates,
have the potential for development but do not undergo it.
Such characters are by definition complex enough to undergo
a shift in the modes of their response; on the whole, their
consciousness must be moderately accessible, and by definition their identities must be more or less coherent as well.
This is why Miss Bates is a better example than Lady
Bertram. In the portrayal of Miss Bates we have a rich if
oblique dramatization of how her blather is part of an
elaborate defense system that serves to ward off intrusion,
contact, and humiliation but also to siphon off whatever
thwarted sexual and maternal energies are bottled up in her.
With Lady Bertram we have virtually no access, even oblique,
to motives and aims.

Miss Bates is a character who seems static but proves
(however minimally) dynamic. There are still other kinds of
characters who are dynamic as well as complex in our
impression and experience of them but who do not develop.
Such characters manifest no significantly shifting structures
of response and no new traits in the course of the action of
the work that generates them. As I noted earlier, Virginia
Woolf's Mrs. Dalloway is a character of this sort, and so to a
lesser degree is Mrs. Ramsay. Both are rendered in terms of a
rich play of conflict, even of doubleness; both convey an
impression of movement, complexity, conflict—in short, dynamism. With both, more is involved than a surface effect of
mere sensibility at play, as Mary McCarthy holds that it
is.[30] The sense of dynamism is created by continuous conflict
and the self-manifestation of truly complex issues in the
heroines' personalities. Yet we feel that Woolf is presenting a
highly stabilized play of conflict, conflict so stabilized that it
precludes change, or development, or even movement toward
meaningful insight in the character. There is some ambiguity
in Mrs. Dalloway's case, to be sure, since the novel that
bears her name builds up to a climax of some force and
urgency: Septimus' death and Mrs. Dalloway's confrontation

with it. Yet the whole structure of the presentation, and the emphases in Mrs. Dalloway's characterization, suggest that we have here a revelation of a stable state rather than a movement toward new insight, or growth within a personality. The end of the novel is so foreshortened that we have little sense that Mrs. Dalloway has integrated the experience she undergoes. At most we have the question of whether she does or does not.

The issue presented by a Mrs. Dalloway in the realm of character creation is a central one, and it involves the question of coherence. The issue, of course, is what we mean by development or change in character and what we mean by its absence. When we say someone changes or develops, do we mean that a new trait has emerged or that something already there has manifested itself? And how do we determine the fine line between the two? In life, where we have endless potential data for establishing whether shifts have occurred, it is possible to uncover possible causes for seemingly "new" behavior, behavior that diverges from our norms of expectation for a particular person or type of person. In literature we often can conjecture what the cause of the new manifestation of character, or at least of desire and loathing, in a character may be, but we often have no firm grounds for validating our conjectures except from within the larger structure of images and events in the work. In this case we work by inference, not from the character's ascertainable system of feelings and motive but from his or her place in the structure of the whole. This, again, is what Janet Adelman does in her reading of Edgar in *King Lear*.[31]

The issues of such change—whether absent, as with Mrs. Dalloway in my view, or relatively contained, as with Miss Bates's manifestation of bruised feelings, or relatively extensive,as with Edmund or Clarissa Harlowe or even Julien Sorel—are complex, and, it should be clear by now, involve several other aspects of character: whether we have access to the character's inner life; whether the character is coherent or not; and whether the character is stylized in a way and a degree that might make the change comprehensible or at least conventionally acceptable. Both extremes of change can involve all of these aspects. We can have the extreme of conversion, verging sometimes on metamorphic transformation—as in Clarissa Harlowe's purging herself of all worldly dross or in Raskolnikov's spiritual regeneration—and the extreme of fixity, as in the tenacious clinging to a psychic, moral, or spiritual position which occurs in Dickens' minor characters or in Ibsen's Brand or Shakespeare's Coriolanus.

Both change and fixity are, however, highly relative qualities. Joseph Gardner, in speaking of Frank Norris and his grotesque characters, notes that Dickens' "fixed" characters derive their relevance and meaning from the hint of flexible response that we glimpse, as in Wemmick's dramatically human personal life with his Aged Parent and Miss Skiffin or Jaggers' hinted sympathy for Molly, Estella, and Pip.[32] Miss Havisham, as I noted earlier, is an extreme case of fluidity manifesting itself within rigidity. Indeed, the distance between the two modes is one of the more problematic aspects of *Great Expectations*, otherwise one of Dickens' most compact and unified novels.

The manifestation of an underlying fluidity or potential dynamism within even the most encrustedly static character is only the extreme surface aspect of something that pervades our consciousness of fixed characters. Within any dynamic psychology, fixity must be perceived as one way of resolving unbearable conflict, as in Freud's view of character as "defense" and Reich's view of "rigidity" and "body armor." However much we refuse to intellectualize or to interpret the dynamics of such conflict in a psychological sense, we experience it as there, or at least potentially there, even when consciousness of it is deflected, as in Dickens' handling of a Wegg or a Pumblechook.

Change may also be perceived as the surface manifestation of a unified or coherent personality. And the coherence involved can, before a moment of final illumination, take the form of extreme rigidity—as in tragic actions, where the hero's ultimate achievement of insight is preceded by actions resulting from blindness and rigidity.

Still, on the whole, we distinguish clearly and sharply between static characters and dynamic ones, and most works operate with a reasonably calibrated scale, ranging from static to dynamic and back again. This is true even of so minimal a form as the fairy tale or folktale and is likely to be more dramatically evident in a complex work. The witch in Grimm's "Hansel and Gretel" is the wicked witch, and that is that. The same is true of the wicked stepmother in this story, who, like the witch, is not only cruel but also orally greedy. Neither figure has any conflict about her ingestive voracity, and neither manifests even a modicum of conflict— of self-doubt, ambivalence, or uncharacteristic desire. The woodcutter is torn by conflict—between self-interest, compounded by fear of his aggressively self-interested wife, and concern for his children. Hansel and Gretel, especially Gretel, not only are full of conflict but also manage to change and grow within the scope of the experience rendered in the tale. They change from the voracious children who get into trouble because of their uncritical assault on the gingerbread house to the prudent manipulators who outwit the witch by shoving her in the oven and then deal with the benign duck at the crossing.[33] There are limits, of course, as I noted in chapter 3, to the attribution of motives to figures in fairy tales, and the limits are imposed by the genre and its conventions. But within those limits, there is a range of possibilities, and that is what concerns me here.[34]

One could bring examples from more complex works to illustrate this principle. The simpler, fairy-tale instance provides a good illustration of a crucial and often obscured fact that I have already noted—namely, that we must beware of equating dynamism with minimal stylization and static character with maximal stylization. Krook, in *Bleak House*, is maximally stylized, and he undergoes the most dramatic change of all: reduction to ash and slime, under the impact of spontaneous combustion. Mrs. Clennam's revival at the end of *Little Dorrit* is another of many examples in Dickens of sudden change.

Bearing such changes in mind, it is worth noting that there is a sense in which it is precisely the comic or grotesque Dickensian or Shakespearean characters that pass through the most extreme metamorphic processes of all. Think of Angelo, in *Measure for Measure*, or parts of the shipwrecked company in *The Tempest*. Characters who are highly stylized and dynamic may, to be sure, not allow us much direct access to their inwardness. For them, the text often provides clear clues to what we may presume to be going on (or to have gone on) within them, as in the imagery of Angelo and Isabella's discourse. On the other hand, characters who are minimally stylized—Hedda Gabler, Miss Julie, even Anna Karenina—give us considerable access to consciousness but, as I noted in my discussion of transparency, may end up deeply mysterious in their ultimate motives, refusing, as people in life often do, to fuse into a simple, vivid, coherent singleness of psychic being.

Closure

Such highly dynamic characters as Anna, Hedda, and Julie—characters whose vital and vivid conflicts stay with us even after they are "dead"—involve us in another dimension of character in literature. I refer to the degree to which the works in which they figure strive to achieve, or in fact achieve, closure in and of the characters they project, and the degree to which the works leave open questions raised by the presentation of their characters. Some characterizations are rigorously closed off at the end of the works in which they figure and are closed off with a finality that admits of no challenge or even speculation. Think, for example, of Oedipus in *Oedipus Rex* and the same character in *Oedipus at Colonus*. From *Rex* to *Colonus* Oedipus develops, yet there is, it seems to me, no ground for questioning the closure of his development by the end of *Oedipus Rex*. Sophocles, however, is quite capable of unresolved closure, as in *Philoctetes*, where the theophany of Herakles does not quite resolve the ambiguity of Philoctetes' attitudes, motives, and choices. The outcome, of course, we know; myth tells us, and the play assures us, that Herakles got to Troy. But the process is hard to envision. Euripides goes much further than Sophocles in undercutting the traditional closure brought about by the god in the machine.

Modern literature is full of such unresolvedness. William James named the issue in his letter to his brother on *The Portrait of a Lady*. After first reading the manuscript of the novel, William complained of the open-endedness of Isabel's fate, which means the ambiguity of her development. Henry, in his response, confirmed that the openness was deliberate, an openness that the novel in fact realized. Such openness or ambiguity is part and parcel of modernity. Is Don Quixote really cured of his delusion? Has Moll Flanders really reformed? Will Stephen Dedalus become a writer? Is Paul Morel released from the world of darkness and death, or is he doomed to be engulfed by it? Will confronting Septimus' death make any mark on Clarissa Dalloway's life? Does Sebastian Knight exist? Has Augie March learned anything? Has Herzog?

The openness or ambiguity of modern texts has its antecedents in the comic tradition, where the happy ending provides a highly conventionalized, deeply qualified means of closure. Will Bertram really reform and love his Helena? Can Orsino really "do" for Olivia? And can the multivalent volatility and repressibility of her libido abate? Feste-Touchstone indirectly suggests that perhaps they cannot, that even in sunny weather we must acknowledge the qualifying negatives: "Hey ho, the wind and the rain." The formal closure of Shakespeare's comedies is marked by a qualification not unlike the one that informs the resolution of his sonnets, where the tidy syllogistic closure of the terminal couplet is undercut by the surge of the dialectic that governs the quatrains that precede it.

Indeed, all highly self-conscious fiction and drama tend to

underscore the factitiousness of the fiction they generate. In doing so, they tend to render problematic the nature and clarity of the characters and their modes of resolving their conflicts. It is this aspect of postmodernist fiction that, as I have noted already, tends to minimize character as a vital aspect of the literary text. When Henry James takes pleasure in challenging us to imagine Isabel as a palpable presence beyond the limits of his novel, he is playing an elaborate illusionistic trick later taken up by such writers as Joyce and Proust—the trick of so vividly animating his character that we envision it in its trajectory beyond the novel in which it figures. This trick is more complex, and in many ways the opposite, of the tendency of nineteenth-century novelists (noted with approval by Chatman) to provide epilogues in which they tuck away the futures of their characters. The epilogue is a strategy of closure, often verging on foreclosure. It tries to head off the possibility of imagining the ongoing life of the characters in the terms accorded them in the body of the novel, though the body of the novel insists, in its specification of tensions, that the closure is a falsification of the characters' reality. Open-endedness, for its part, may be a strategy for inviting us to envision more than the novel has time to tell us.

The difference between open-endedness and closure has to do with the extent to which a writer resolves the conflicts that the characters are subject to and makes those resolutions coincide with the patterning of events in the plot. Obviously, writers can signify ambiguity and openness—can even provide trick and alternative endings. Brecht plays with this strategy frequently, and Dickens beguiles us with it in his ambivalence about his revised ending to *Great Expectations*. Those who do so deliberately strive to tease us into factoring alternative possibilities. Whatever the motive, however, in the end openness rests on deliberate lack of resolution, closure on the tidy working out of elements.

5

Kinds of Characters,
Kinds of Texts

It should be clear by now that despite my espousal of Chatman's static paradigm of traits as a way of conceptualizing character, and despite the relatively static aspects of my taxonomy, I take a highly dynamic view of character in both literature and life. Such a view not only defines character in life as an emergent structure arising from a complex play of conflict in the individual; it also conceives of character in literature as part of a highly dynamic, if also stabilized, structure. That structure presents us with the process of coming into being at two levels. First there is the text itself, which generates images of characters by unfolding the materials of which we constitute them. Second there is the character, which as an imagined entity comes into being and falls out of being as it responds to the circumstances—to events and to other characters—delineated in the text. The latter process is what interests me here. It involves the character's recurrent rediscovery and reintegration of its own qualities—or its failure to do so. Such process in character is projected within verbal, narrative, and dramatic structures that are finely adapted to its needs.

Indeed, there is a close fit between process as projected in character and the process of a literary work's own unfolding.

That coordination rests on the inherently dynamic nature of the literary work. The dynamism of character in its various aspects is a dimension of the dynamic nature of literary texts as explicit or implicit narratives—that is, as articulated story, as in epics, folktales, comedies, or novels; as incipient story, as in lyric poems, which imply situations that may be expanded into narratives; or as character sketches, such as Theophrastus', that also suggest situations and seem ready to unfurl themselves into actions.

In principle, it may be said that to arrange events in sequence, as stories do, is to imply a connection between the events. Since there is no point, except as a self-conscious literary-metaphysical joke, in arranging identical or impossible events in sequence, stories ordinarily imply process, the process, at least, of getting from one event to another. E. M. Forster implies this in his categorical division of narratives into "story"—a sequence of events linked by "and then's" —and "plot"—a sequence of events linked causally. (Forster's examples are, for story, "The king died and then the queen died," as contrasted with, for plot, "The king died and then the queen died of grief.") Thus narrative invokes the aspects of change (or development) and causality implied by ordinary sequence.[1]

Any sequence of events implies process, the process of things leading to each other and following from each other. Not all sequences imply the same kind or degree of process, and not all sequences imply process or development in characters. Indeed, texts are not uniform in the way they handle time and render process, and one of the pivotal preoccupations of twentieth-century critical theory has been to explore the place of time in fiction and its implication for the overall structure of literary works.

Edwin Muir was one of the pioneers in this area, and his study *The Structure of the Novel* was a seminal work that tried to distinguish between texts structured in terms of space and those that are organized in terms of time. The one, Muir held, tends to be static and social, the other dynamic and tragic. Space-centered novels, he held, render a scene and contain spatialized characters, characters that are organized paradigmatically; that is, in terms of traits that constellate in a static way to form a pattern largely unaffected by time and experience. Time novels render a sequence and contain characters who undergo experience in time; time, in a manner of speaking, passes through them and consumes them. Hence, according to Muir, the difference between static and dynamic characters. The first are not subject to time and therefore not subject to change; the second are victims of time and therefore undergo dramatic changes.[2]

As Muir himself insisted, texts do not line up neatly as space- or time-centered entities. Indeed, the concept of space-centeredness in the novel, especially, is a very relative one.[3] In principle, as Joseph Frank has suggested in rejecting his own earlier notion of spatial form as the defining quality of the modern novel, there are no spatial texts, only relatively spatializing ones. Yet the way in which the latter novels evoke process in character is very different from the way in which time-centered novels do so.[4] Beyond that, even time-centered texts are not of a piece from any point of view, and certainly not with regard to character. In both kinds of text, any consideration of the nature and quality of character and of the kind of process that characters embody must take at least two other crucial elements into account. One is the extent to which character is central to the text; the other is the extent to which the action that the text embodies is itself centralized, unified, and time-oriented.[5] If character is central to the text and the action is highly unified, then it follows that the character is likely to be more complex and dynamic; that is, subject to development, and even change. If character is not foregrounded within the text, or if the action is not unified (as in certain folktales or, among post-Renaissance genres, in the picaresque novel), then character will tend to be more static and simple.

The most extreme case of the latter phenomenon is the text that contains no action and hence no time dimension. In

Theophrastus' "characters," for example, characters are central; each text is designed to reveal a kind of character. But the character types are presented in nonsequences of events, in disparate situations that are not unified by any story and not linked in sequential relations to the other texts. Hence there is no unfolding interaction within the causal sequence of events, and the character revealed "is," rather than "becomes."

A similar principle is at work in picaresque actions, where, despite the presence of temporal sequences and therefore of possibly meaningful process, the protagonist is ordinarily denied meaningful relationships with the characters who confront him in the episodic structure of the story.[6] Failing to engage and doomed to incessant manipulation, the ordinary picaro, even when he has very marked traits, often does not emerge as a coherent figure. Paradoxically, such characters generally have only a limited number of traits, expressed in a pattern of relatively automatistic repetition, with no significant variations. The characters within tightly knit comic plots, for their part, are highly schematized, and their traits are often very varied. But such characters tend not to be dynamic, because the action works independently of them; they may be central to the action, but the process of their engagement with the other characters involved in it is not foregrounded and is not directly exposed to the reader. In the picaresque narrative, episodic structure tends to block meaningful causal sequences and hence to circumvent process, which is evoked neither by the action nor in the character. In compact, classical comic structures, process may be richly evoked, but not in ways that ordinarily implicate character or dramatize process within it.

At the other pole, in tragedy and in what Muir calls the dramatic novel, the protagonist tends to stand at the center of the action and tends to stand in a posture of engagement with the characters and circumstances that confront him or her. Most of all, the protagonist is not only foregrounded but engaged with others within the time process of the action. Such a character's process of response is, moreover, exposed in one degree or another and is therefore accessible to us. Compared to that of static characters, the process of the protagonist's response tends to be continuous or at least coherent. Even when the tragic character loses coherence for a while, as in *Othello* or *Lear*, we are ordinarily asked both to contemplate the restoration of coherence and to experience the grounds of that coherence, convincing or unconvincing, as the case may be.[7] As Muir points out, comic structures like *Pride and Prejudice* are capable of similar effects, but less commonly so.[8]

Aristotle's treatment of the development of tragedy in the *Poetics* illuminates both the factor of involvement among characters and the element of sequence, implying time, in the generation of character. Aristotle notes that Thespis separated the protagonist, who was presumably played by an actor, from the chorus; that Aeschylus added a second actor; and that Sophocles added a third.[9] The development from Aeschylus to Sophocles—and, even within Aeschylus, from *The Suppliant Maidens* through *The Oresteia*—is, among other things, a development from rigid, relatively monolithic (though conflict-ridden) characterization to characterizations of increasing subtlety and flexibility. This is so, it seems to me, partly because of the greater field for the interplay of challenge and response among three figures than among two, especially when, as in Greek tragedy, represented discourse is public. More response potentially means more faceting, and more faceting means a greater possible field for the rendering of conflict. Interaction among a multiplicity of characters need not generate engagement and revelation; witness the space-centered novel such as *Vanity Fair*, which animates a vast cast of characters for purposes other than the presentation of process in character. Conversely, dialogue between two characters, especially in intimate situations, as between Shakespeare's Antony and Cleopatra, can evoke rich and subtle interactions. In principle, absence of engaged interactions, public or private, makes it difficult to evoke experience or inner process in characters.

Aristotle's pinpointing of reversal as the pivot of tragic

action highlights the time element—or rather the sequence element—as the medium of the process that narrative implies.[10] Again, time and its sequences are the medium of change; without time there is no change, and without change or the possibility of change there is no dynamism in character. Aristotle's emphasis on recognition as the sequel to reversal in the sequence of the tragic plot stresses the relation of temporal process to character.[11] It foregrounds the fact that in tragedy at least, the progression of events in the play evokes response and therefore stirs process in character. The recognition of what has happened in the reversal and of the role of the character in what has happened makes for an integration or incorporation of process—even of seemingly external fate-filled process—in character.

One of the curious aspects of literary works, as of life situations, is that it is the narrow rather than the broad span of time that is the common medium of dramatically perceptible dynamism in character. The most dynamic and conflict-ridden characters, those subject to the most highly dramatized sense of process, tend to be those who, like Anna Karenina, Raskolnikov, and Othello, figure in works that focus largely on present actions and therefore possess relatively shallow time dimensions. Such characters tend to be engaged with events that follow from their choices in the present action. The dynamism of the works in which they figure tends to flow directly from the conflict between such characters and the people they engage or challenge; the dynamism of the characters stems from the disequilibration of the unresolved or faultily resolved elements within them. But it also stems from the ordering of events in sequences that imply the organization of time, even when no major time warps are included.

Process-filled works with shallow time dimensions should not be seen as lacking in time tension—that is, in tension between things that have already happened and things that happen at any subsequent moment of the action. In such works, the time tension within the limited time span of the action may be considerable because it is compressed, conflict-ridden, and more or less directly present to consciousness throughout. The paradigm used by Francis Fergusson for describing tragic rhythm and tragic form is useful in this regard. In Fergusson's view, the tragic rhythm is generated by a sequence of experience that he sums up as "purpose, passion, perception." In his formulation, what is involved in tragedy is a purposive effort by a protagonist who, as he acts to achieve his purpose, elicits opposition and generates conflict. As a result, the protagonist is rent by conflict and suffering ("passion") until, at the end of his trajectory, ne arrives at perception, which is the Aristotelian *anagnorisis* around which he consolidates his consciousness. Within that trajectory, the action moves forward by a series of conflicts, with others and with self, with the protagonist engaging others and being engaged by others at every step of the way.[12]

The tension is between what has taken place within the span of the present action and what is taking place now, at whatever later moment; between Anna Karenina as she was when we first glimpsed her on the train pulling into Moscow and Anna as she is when she goes to the train station and kills herself; between Othello as he was in his speech before the Venetian Senate and Othello as he is when he rolls on the floor, screaming, "Goats and monkeys!" or when, in a haze of self-righteousness, he throttles Desdemona; and so on. In each case, we are invited to fill in the spaces—the "gaps" —between one moment, one image, and the next, and to fill them in with appropriate detail as to motive and as to the whole configuration of the personality as it moves from one state of being and feeling to another.[13]

One curious thing about works with shallow time perspectives is that they tend to provide only small amounts of life-historical information. Even when they elaborate themselves on the scale of a large novel, as in *Anna Karenina* or *Middlemarch*, the emphasis is likely to be on the characters' responsiveness to the immediate, the given situation. Hence the acuteness of the problem of the life history of character in literature. The most vividly available characters tend to be intensely engaged in the immediate circumstances of the actions that generate them. In this sense, the synecdochic aspect of character generation figures here, much as in the creation of the Wife of Bath; the glimpsed part, or fragment, effectively stands for the whole.

The embodied presence of the characters as glimpsed even at their first appearance implicitly contains—as a first glimpse of a person in life may do, though perhaps less vividly—the whole process of their development. We are ordinarily impelled to intuit this development, without much specification of detail, on the basis of the experiences we see the characters undergo in the course of the work. We assume that the experiences, responses, and conflicts that they have in the present action epitomize their characteristic modes of experience at all times and that the structure of values and choices which makes them what they are in the present reflects what they were in the past. Yet the amount of sheer information given is generally very limited, considering the richness of the impression they make.

Works with deep time perspectives would seem to have a larger scope for suggesting process than those with shallow ones. As with shallow time perspective, of course, the kind of character generated depends on the centrality of the character to the action in which it is found; on the degree of its engagement with the world around it; on the quality of consciousness in it; and on the text's concern with character, consciousness, and motivation. In principle, however, radical time warps in the displacement of *fabula* into *syujhet* or story into discourse—that is, the "chronological" sequence of events, taken from the earliest recounted event, as opposed to the sequence in which events are actually given in the text—do provide a rich field for evoking the kind of process characters undergo. Such process often seems analogous to what people suffer over long periods in life.

Faulkner's "A Rose for Emily" and Dickens' *Great Expectations* exemplify two extremes of formal wrenching of sequence, wrenching that generates deep time perspective and serves as a vehicle for the time themes of the texts. They seem worth considering in relative detail because of the way in which their time perspectives and time warps operate, both in themselves and in relation to other modes.

"A Rose for Emily" skews the natural or historical sequence of events in such a way as initially to fix our consciousness on an image of Emily as she is in later life, but with constant reference to various moments of her experience in the past. The image with which we begin is presented as it has crystallized rather late in the "story," in the diffuse consciousness of her small-town community; it is projected by an unparticularized, unindividualized, virtually undramatized narrative voice that identifies with that consciousness. The voice tells us of Miss Emily's oddness, of her withdrawal, of her impoverishment, of her fierce pride, of her hostility to change and to the demands of a changing world. We hear of her rigidity, of how she exists in fixity, "like an idol," as she stares out the window. The elements of her past that are presented to us (such as the "tableau" in which her father horsewhips a suitor; her engagement; and her fiancé's disappearance) suggest a link between the conditions that led to her thwarting as a marriageable aristocratic southern girl and the estrangement, fixity, rage, and inscrutability of her being at the end of her life, with which the story begins. Disclosure of the final horror—the image of her fiancé's skeleton decked out in wedding clothes with Emily's gray pigtail on the pillow alongside it—heightens curiosity about the events of the past, and the logic of those events, the psycho-logic that led her to do whatever she did and to become what she is.

"A Rose for Emily" leaves us with a "global gap," an insoluble mystery. All imaginable construings of the text cannot tell us just what happened or why. Yet central to the story is a cluster of possibilities, any one of which might supply an explanation of Emily's process of becoming what she has become. None of them, however, can be validated. Did she kill Homer Barron because he did sleep with her or because he didn't? If he had slept with her, was it the pleasure or the pain of it that goaded her? And so on, ad nauseam. What is curious about all possibilities that crop up is that they all can factor within our understanding of Emily; each of them sustains and is explicated by the structure of images through which the essential Emily is projected.[14]

As a result, our sense of Emily remains multiply ambiguous. The image we retain of her remains both rigid and fluid. It is rigid in her specific and final incarnation, fluid in our sense of the processes that may have led her to be what that image implies. In effect, we find ourselves entertaining a set of superimposed and sometimes dissonant images and processes. The effect is like that which I have already noted with regard to Moll Flanders, with the difference that here the text provides us with tentative keys to the various riddles but no consolidation of meaning in the character's consciousness, which remains utterly opaque, and no possible disambiguation of possibilities in our own. Indeed, in the multiplicity of keys and motives she is more like Shakespeare's protagonists than like Moll, since in Shakespeare's tragic figures comprehensive motivational possibilities tend to present themselves and even to be supported by a variety of materials in the text. In Emily Grierson, Moll, and Shakespeare's protagonists, we are challenged to seek an ordering of motives that might bestow coherence upon the traits and motives the character presents to our consciousness. That challenge seems to me closely analogous to the challenge posed in life of understanding the motives for things that people do seemingly without cause. Emily is interesting because of the specifically twentieth-century way in which the complexities of motivation are conveyed through very deliberate, self-conscious manipulation of time sequence, voice, and focalization. The fact that Faulkner's manipulation of time is probably motivated at least in part by a historical and sociological interest—namely, the presentation of Emily as a scion of the Old South and as a victim of its mores—does not detract from the fact that it serves to create a shifting field of motivational elements. Indeed, it generates useful elements within that field in its heaping up of sociohistoric factors that contribute to Emily's state of mind and being.

Emily Grierson, as a character generated in a text with deep time dimensions, is doubly interesting in juxtaposition with Miss Havisham in *Great Expectations*. At first glance Miss Havisham seems very like Emily in her fixity, her thwartedness, her aggressiveness. On closer examination, she proves to be both presented and motivated in significantly different ways. In *Great Expectations*, we start with a set of stylized, static impressions of Miss Havisham, impressions still more opaque than those we initially have of Emily. As the past emerges, however, we grasp the process through which Miss Havisham has come to be what she is. As I noted in my discussion of dynamism and opacity, the main action of the novel, set in the present and moving toward revelation of the past, presents a process that Miss Havisham, like Pip, undergoes before our very eyes. As Pip moves toward self-discovery and discovery of the reality and value of others, we learn why Miss Havisham became a bitter recluse but also that she has changed from what she was at the beginning of the novel. That is, we see how she becomes a suffering human being, vulnerable to the emotions that she has striven to shut out in her life. Not only is the crucial gap—why Miss Havisham is as she is, why her clock is stopped at twenty to nine, why she wears her decaying bridal gown—closed, but in closing it Dickens gives us a schematic derivation for Miss Havisham's character, an etiology confirmed by the development she undergoes in the course of the present action. That etiology is underscored by the fact that we see Miss Havisham herself arrive at consciousness of its implications for her life in the present action.

The firm derivation of her condition presents a dramatic contrast to the obscurity of Emily's history and development.

"A Rose for Emily" facets its information to heighten our sense of the indeterminacy and complexity of the process that made Emily what she is. We have, in her presentation, the kind of flicker effect that, as I note earlier in connection with Moll and Shakespeare's tragic heroes, elicits a variety of speculations provisionally confirmable from within the text. Its strategy of presentation solicits speculation on our part. *Great Expectations* does the opposite. It obstructs speculation by motivating behavior in a single-minded way. We would become pointlessly tangled in hopeless questions if we asked whether Miss Havisham deliberately decided to withdraw from the world or if we considered her domestic arrangements— how her household ran—during the decades of withdrawal and decay. Not so with Emily. We are solicited to wonder whether her servant was privy to all that went on in the house and to ponder the implications of the various possible answers.

Yet we are nonetheless asked to apprehend a large psychological trajectory for Miss Havisham. We are asked to do so in the context of imagery (decaying wedding cake, bugs, stopped clocks, shuttered windows) that explicates the emotional logic of her immurement in richly revealing terms. This pattern of images does not dramatize process, does not suggest what may have gone on in any present moment along the trajectory of action. Rather it presents a highly schematic pattern, a kind of psychological paradigm that elucidates her condition in a stabilized way, from which we can infer process but not its unfolding, as we can obliquely in "A Rose for Emily." I shall return at the end of this chapter to the issue of such spatializable patterns and their use in the creation of character. Here what needs to be noted is that the way in which the deep time dimensions and the confluence of past and present within the text are organized implies the considerable development Miss Havisham has undergone and pointedly asks us to contemplate it—much as "A Rose for Emily" points us to the question of how Emily got that way.

Texts can handle configurations of time, sequence, and confrontation in a great variety of ways and can achieve wildly different effects in the generation of character by doing so. Often several strategies are used in the same text, contributing to its complexity. In *Middlemarch*, for example, we have an illuminating variety of actions—at least four major actions and several subsidiary ones—that echo and counterpoint each other in both formal and substantive ways, and the time and sequence aspect of the text is at least as complex as the other aspects. Like Pip (and like most nineteenth-century ingénues), Dorothea exists in a present action that contains very few backward glances and that gives us very little information about the past. Dorothea's experience in the present action accumulates and, until Casaubon's death at least, adds up. But it does not dredge up much that matters from her past; what is presented is presented at the outset as a given of her character—her life in the Swiss pension, for example, or her Protestantism, or the conflict within her between sensuality and asceticism. Dorothea engages with people, however, who have more detailed and sometimes more manifestly meaningful pasts, pasts that bear on the present action of the novel. Her interaction with them elicits a sense of her as a person with a complex life history, providing us with considerable insight but little information.

For the others, the progress of the action often unearths both insight and information. Casaubon is presented vividly at the beginning and proves to be compulsively driven by repressed needs and suppressed rage; the unfolding of his responses in the present action throws up a set of images that pointedly suggest the structure of his unconscious life. That life consists not of specific events, as with Miss Emily or Miss Havisham, but rather of loaded circuits of feeling, feeling that in the end constricts, congests, and destroys him. Lydgate, too, though to a far lesser degree than Casaubon, has an obscured past. This is not his childhood, of which we are given an account at the outset, in the presentation of his character, but rather his affair with "that divine cow," Laure. When Rosamund's deadly coerciveness and tenacity—the qualities that lead Lydgate to speak of her at the end of his life as "a basil plant that feeds on dead men's brains"—get the best of him, we are in possession of a suggestive key to his victimizability. An obscure but climactic detail from his past, given in the course of a coherent early presentation of his life before his arrival at Middlemarch, has been waiting to illuminate his drama of defeat in his heroic dream of achievement in science. Bulstrode, for his part, is overtaken by his past even as he grinds away at his machinations in the present action.

A useful as well as moving aspect of George Eliot's complicated time scheme and her no less complex handling of the issue of time is the way she exemplifies different possibilities of relating past to present in the life of her characters and of engaging (or not engaging) them directly with what the past coughs up. Not only does each of the main characters have a different time-depth dimension, but each one relates to that dimension in a different way. Lydgate, Bulstrode, and Casaubon, all of whom are seen in relation to their significant pasts, refuse in varying degrees to arrive at consciousness of the past and of its relation to their present lives and values. Of Lydgate it is directly said that he is one of those men who will be slowly eroded, so that one day he will move among the "furniture, like a ghost" of his former self. Of Casaubon, it need not be said he is a ghost; his intrinsic ghostliness and his association with the buried and the dead evoke the image throughout. And Bulstrode is, in a manner of speaking, overtaken by a ghost, the ghost of a past that he has tried to bury. That past rises up in the person of Raffles to lay its "dead hand" upon him and destroy the facade of righteousness that he has presented to the Middlemarch world. Bulstrode, too, does not seem to integrate the whole range of his past actions, with all their implications and complications, in his consciousness. Only Dorothea does that, and compared to the others she has had a very limited specified past to deal with by the time the novel ends. But deal with it she does.

In *Middlemarch*, each of the main characters undergoes a different kind of process. That process is directly related to the narrative's organization of each character's experience in terms of time and sequence, as well as its presentation of the quality and degree of consciousness of which the character is capable. In *Middlemarch* George Eliot uses several modes of confrontation and several methods of organizing time and sequence to evoke process in character. Those ways are culled from a variety of literary genres, which manipulate time schemes, consciousness, and causality in different ways.

The Bulstrode action echoes both classical (as opposed to novelistic) romance and the tragedy of fate. In each of these genres, elaborate chains of events, constituting a decisive causal system, come to bear on the protagonist, with the difference that in tragedy (*Oedipus Rex* is a prime example) the protagonist confronts the chains of causality outside the sphere of his deliberate choices and assumes responsibility for them, while in romance and in comedy the protagonist tends neither to confront nor to integrate what emerges but only to float on the positive consequences of what he learns about his nature, his identity, and his experience. In novelistic romance, the affinity is with tragedy and unhappy endings, but without the dramatization of consciousness that tragedy allows. As I noted in chapter 3, a romance such as *Wuthering Heights* relies very heavily on imagery and patterning devices to communicate the meaning of the characters' experience.

The Dorothea action, on the other hand, operates in ways that are typical of what has sometimes been called "tragedy of character." Such tragedy should be so designated not because, as some have held, some "flaw" in the character of the protagonist caused the tragedy, making it imperative for him to bear its consequences, but rather because in the present action the character is engaged in confronting the circumstances of its life and is therefore revealed in the course of it. Not only Dorothea, in *Middlemarch*, but also Anna Karenina and Maggie Verver in the novel and

Shakespeare's tragic protagonists in the drama undergo such a present process of confrontation, response, and development.

I am not quite sure how to designate the kind of action that Casaubon and Lydgate inhabit, but it seems to me they are involved in something akin to novelistic romance on the one hand and ironic comedy on the other. The sense of being overtaken by a ghost, which I described earlier, is reminiscent of the Gothic modes of romance, with their elicitation of pasts that are not specified but rather evoked as manifestations of opaque unconscious process. "The Fall of the House of Usher" is typical of this, with its upsurge of a presence from a deep, dynamite-laden vault. Ironic comedy, such as *Measure for Measure*, also fits here in its tendency to dramatize opaque processes of development in which characters arrive at little or no awareness of what is going on with them and the audience arrives at very little more.

One decisive element in the presentation of character in the context of action is the kind of consciousness and conflict conferred upon it. Stories with a considerable depth of past time that bears on the present action, such as "A Rose for Emily" and *Great Expectations*, have a built-in potential for process and dynamism, but they need not realize that potential and need not render either process or dynamism with any degree of concreteness. In this they are like classical romance. Whether they realize their potential for rendering process or not depends on the inwardness of the characters. What saves Iphigenia at Tauris is not anything that goes on within her but rather the mechanical working out of time, event, and divine intervention. The difference between Sophocles' Oedipus, Ibsen's Solness, or even Arthur Miller's Willy Loman and the protagonists of romance is the former characters' relatively greater capacity to confront and integrate experience and their readiness to do so.

With regard to consciousness, the range of possibilities is vast. Different kinds of text and different kinds of characters have different kinds and amounts of consciousness. Modes of consciousness are developed in conformity both with the kind of characters involved and with their function in the texts that generate them.

What I wish to stress here, however, is the fact that a great range of temporal or sequential orderings, as well as of focalizations, figures in the projection of characters with very varied modes of consciousness. Gérard Genette's categories for the analysis of such dimensions seem to me indispensable. They are easily the best we have for classifying and analyzing the patterning of events, in and out of sequence, in stories; for specifying whether something happened before, during, or after the inception of the ongoing action; and for specifying the consciousness through which we contemplate the information that emerges in the course of any ongoing action.[15] Their usefulness lies in establishing the patterns of confrontation within any text insofar as the protagonist is a center of consciousness and confronts the implications of his actions and feelings.

One could use Genette's conceptual structure to go him one better by working out ratios for the relationship between time dimensions and modes not only of focalization but of consciousness. I do not intend to attempt this here; I wish to note only the fact that a variety of ratios is possible and that literature in all times has used a considerable range of such possibilities, though the literature of our century has gone to especially great lengths to explore options.

Thus, Virginia Woolf uses a curious pattern of time and consciousness patterns in *Mrs. Dalloway,* not to suggest a process of development in character but rather to lay out the given—the unchanging though stress-filled play of tension in a character who is revealed as she is, rather than presented in the process of change. *Mrs. Dalloway,* with its Clarissa plot, shuttles between two different points in time. There is the now, in which Clarissa plans and gives her party, and the then, which is that summer at Bourton when she rejected Peter, was kissed by Sally, and decided to marry Richard Dalloway. Mrs. Dalloway, but Peter too, lives in dramatic relation to that past time, not confronting it. There is, to my mind, no significant confrontation, despite the impression of climactic reaching toward it when Clarissa learns of Septimus' death, but merely a recurrent remembering of it and evoking of it. That shuttling back and forth in time is counterpointed against the movement back and forth in space, in present time, from Clarissa to Septimus to Peter, which also gives rise to no significant confrontations.

Analogous but very different kinds of time juxtapositions figure in Proust and Faulkner. In Proust they appear to evoke the elusiveness of experience; in Faulkner they tend to evoke such effects as those achieved in "A Rose for Emily": that is, an effect of development and unfolding, over long spans of time, with little specification of motive or other characterological elements.

Certain modern works, in the tradition of the novelistic exploration of time shift, play with time in other ways that relate to character. *Death of a Salesman*, for example, though clearly not a wildly experimental work, intersperses past and present in a curious and effective way. Borrowing the device of flashback with "dissolve" from the movies, it presents its action in terms of the intrusion of past events into Willy's consciousness as pressures on him in the present action mount unbearably. The strategy is different from that of *Hamlet* and *Macbeth*, where supernatural agencies erupt into the present action, partly because the eruptions are clearly the intrusion of past events, as they "really" happened, and as they might surface into consciousness. It is different from the strategy of traditional drama with a deep time dimension— say, *Oedipus Rex*—in that instead of information about the past being spoken by characters who communicate with each other on the stage, scenes from the past are directly enacted onstage.[16] The effect is different, chiefly because we have a more highly charged (dramatized) presentation of the impact of the past on the present. In *Death of a Salesman*, this serves to denote with considerable specificity the unfolding of a complex, destructive oedipal pattern within the family, an unfolding that bears on all the people involved and that involves radical, even fatal changes.

Yet *Death of a Salesman*, like many other modern works that play elaborately with time sequences, is not primarily a drama of consciousness, any more than "A Rose for Emily" is a tale of consciousness. We note again that the evocation and exploration of psychic process and human responsiveness need not be mediated through the consciousness of the character. Consciousness figures centrally in the kind of essentially present-tense action that has a Dorothea Brooke, an Anna Karenina, or an Othello for its protagonist; it also figures, but in very different ways, in the kind of retrospective narrative of consciousness that we find in Proust. Even tragedies that have a late point of attack and therefore, on the whole, relatively deep time perspectives (*Oedipus Rex, Ghosts*) —tragedies that contain dramatic reversals and move toward confrontation with events and motives in the past—do not necessarily stress the development and even the elaborated exposure of consciousness. For reasons of its own, the Proustian retrospective narrative tends to lack a centralizing, dramatized present action within which to place the retrospective detail. Hence the absence in the text, and for the reader or viewer, of climactic movements of perception such as most readers have seen as central to the tragic form.

Indeed, all of the kinds of temporal and sequential organization that the moderns and the postmoderns have experimented with ad nauseam allow for the possibility of minimal consciousness in the characters, and especially—what is my main concern here—minimal *integrated* consciousness. *Mrs. Dalloway*, for example, is a novel of consciousness, but one of its salient features is the fact that the rhythm of consciousness in its characters is intermittent. This is a decisive aspect of its formal articulation; it renders consciousness elaborately, but in a state of considerable dissociation. The novel is highly organized, in terms of its images and structures of analogy among characters. But the characters themselves are not highly organized in their awareness of themselves, and the novel itself moves toward no climactic moments of awareness and of confrontation with the implications of awareness.

Yet even in works where consciousness is maximal and the process of arriving at consciousness is central to the work, it is often clear that characters never reach the comprehensive degree of consciousness that is offered to the reader or viewer. Hume's skepticism with regard to identity is again relevant in this context, in the sense that even in moments of climactic synthesis of experience and of clashing views of themselves it is impossible for these characters to synthesize all the elements of their being. This is true even for moments, such as the moment of "perception" in tragedy, that look back to all the other moments along the way.

It is not only for the character, moreover, that experience does not necessarily add up conclusively. For the reader or viewer, too, the temporality of texts and of the process they imply makes it hard to apprehend and combine all of the elements of experience that a character undergoes. The situation is like the one that Percy Lubbock describes with reference to all narrative works. It stems from the fact that the span of time that their texts represent makes it difficult to hold a narrative work simultaneously in our minds.[17] Chatman's concept of a paradigm of traits can be useful in this respect; however problematically, it legitimates the tendency to abstract, schematize, and stabilize—indeed, to render static—the dynamic process of experience.

Highly spatializing texts make this process easier by presenting us with relatively, though often only apparently, static characters: characters who may in principle or potentially be complex and capable of dynamism and development, but who are presented in a highly static, schematic, and spatialized set of images and traits. Dickens' grotesques are an extreme case of such characterization, but most grotesques in literature work in this way. The grotesque character, in literature as in life, is seen to undergo little experience; one might say that the amount of lived experience that a grotesque *person* experiences is in inverse relation to the signs he or she gives of experience. But the experience—or conflict—that such a person undergoes tends to be highly schematized in its forms of self-manifestation, and therefore relatively easy to grasp and interpret.

For example, in Dickens the combination of traits—verbal and gustatory—in a Mr. Micawber is manifested at a single glance; all the behavioral variations upon them merely serve to reinforce the scheme on which Mr. Micawber's character and characterization are based. Yet, as I have already noted with reference to Mr. Woodhouse, the static schematism of Mr. Micawber is no simpler in its psycho-logic and is potentially no less dynamic than the schematism of dynamic characters. The structure of his character is just more evident and more simultaneous in its presentation. The pattern of qualities that is Mr. Micawber is directly made up of his verbal floridities and orotundities; of his feckless assumption that life will provide; of his bibulous and gustatory propensities. Indirectly, the figuration of his immediate family and environment reinforces the schematic reading of his character and motives. His wife always has a baby at the breast; one of the twins is always taking "liquid refreshment." And his bulbous appearance further supports the sense of awkward, fear-filled, infantile vulnerability.

Mr. Micawber, like Dickens' other grotesques, "bubbles up," as Virginia Woolf puts it, with instant vitality; he is generated, it would seem, in a single stroke.[18] The instantaneousness of his generation, however, is not a matter of spontaneous generation on Dickens' part but of immediate apprehension on the reader's part. Such apprehension is made possible by the inherently spatialized, paradigmatic schematism of their generation. We call them "caricatures" of human beings because they bear a resemblance to the caricature, a kind of simplified picture that we take in at a glance.

In psychological terms we may call Mr. Micawber an example of arrested development, a development that remains fixed and helpless at some early stage of growth. All literary grotesques lend themselves to "reading" in this way; so do all human grotesques—that is, persons in life who present a constellation of exaggerated, obsessive, or repetitive qualities. In life as in literature the poverty of experience in the grotesque can be explained in terms of such fixation or arrest. Such poverty of experience does not mean simplicity of structure, however. It means, for the observer at least, simultaneity or instantaneity of perception.

It means, moreover, the evidence of the scheme. Mr. Micawber is more manifestly a "paradigm of traits" than Anna Karenina. In him, the absence of visible process, the arrest of his development within the present world of the text in which he appears, is a function of the absence of process in the segment of the narrative structure that generates him. Because the principle of his response in any situation is nonresponse—or rather, mechanical response—we do not have to undergo the process of inferring his traits from behavior. Nor must we undergo the complex and often elusive process of combining into a single pattern the traits (perhaps contradictory) that accumulate from "observation" of his behavior in a variety of situations. Unlike dynamic characters, he is "given" at the outset. Process may, from a psychological point of view, be frozen or deflected within his response system. But in terms of our experience of him, process might as well not be there. His automatism saves us the emphatic struggle to make him out. He is, despite all the implicit complexity, all the conflict that is presumably buried within him, ready-made. Hence, too, the aptness of the static quality of his summing up as a paradigm.

Absence of process in the ongoing behavior and experience of a Mr. Micawber is a function of an absence of process in the narrative context that generates him. *David Copperfield*, the novel, purports to set out a process. That process is manifestly David's own growth and accommodation to a constructive role in the world. Micawber and his family play no part in that process. They are fixed elements in the human environment that David passes through, the equally

fixed elements in the symbolic field that sets out and inter-
prets the meaning of his growth. One sign of this is the fact
that the Micawbers themselves are not involved in active
relationships that imply, causal sequences that can produce
change.

Micawber, to be sure, does "change" toward the end of the
novel. One sign of his doing so is the way in which he is
drawn into the pattern of the action that leads to the defeat of
Uriah Heep, the restoration of Mr. Wickfield, and David's
marriage to Agnes. But that change is not a development, not
a manifestation of any comprehensible dynamism within
Micawber. Rather, it is an exigency of the plot that makes
him other than he was, that turns him into something else in
a way that even Anna Karenina's radical transformation does
not change her. Mr. Micawber's character becomes incoherent and opaque when he changes, or "develops"—when he
shows dynamism.

Absence of comprehensible process in the Mr. Micawber
we imagine is one of the qualities that makes it so difficult, if
not impossible, to imagine him as the central figure in a
novel. Insofar as narratives imply process, extremely static,
schematic characters tend not to figure as their protagonists.
The structure of Dickens' novels confirms this principle.
Their protagonists—often the least interesting and vivid characters in them—are ordinarily dynamic in form and capable of
development, though they are also on the whole shallow,
uninteresting, and unconvincing, especially when we are
asked to believe that they change or develop. Indeed, the
closer we come to the center of the action in a Dickens novel,
the less static and stylized the characters tend to be; the
farther from the center we move, the more static, stylized,
and grotesque the characters will be and the more simultaneous their mode of presentation. Since the dynamism of the
protagonists is not densely or vividly rendered, the flanking
static figures must be the vehicle for our understanding (but
not our experience) of the process within the central figures.
The flanking figures serve emblematically to externalize and

objectify what may be presumed to be going on within the protagonists. Uriah Heep, Steerforth, and Micawber function in this way as flanking figures for David Copperfield.[19]

As I noted in chapter 4, static figures need not be grotesque, blatantly schematic, extremely stylized, or initially opaque. Odysseus does not change in the course of the *Odyssey*, just as Mrs. Dalloway does not change or develop in the course of the novel that bears her name. The schematism of Odysseus' character, moreover, is no more obvious than that of Anna Karenina or Emma Bovary; it must be inferred from the manifold situations of the *Odyssey*. Indeed, we cannot know how static Odysseus' character in fact is till we reach the end of the epic and can assess its coherence. Part of Homer's strategy in the *Odyssey* is to create the impression of dynamism and movement, to give us false leads and blinds, so as to divert attention from certain of Odysseus' constant traits.[20] Odysseus, moreover, is potentially dynamic. He has not only the surface play of responsiveness that, like Mrs. Dalloway's, creates the illusion of movement and generates a sense of the reality of his responses and of his responsive*ness;* he also, we feel, could "change" in response to challenges. He is like certain kinds of real people in that we feel, as we observe him, the integral availability of his own "being" in response to circumstances. In his case such availability involves especially the ability to cope, as he buckles or toughens in response to extreme circumstances.

Odysseus is an interesting case because of the felt potential for change in his character and because of the lack of highly schematizing stylization in his presentation. He is also interesting, and typical of a certain kind of static character, in that he figures at the center of an action that involves process. Indeed, the *Odyssey* is in some way about process—about the potential impact of time, events, and experience on people, relationships, and institutions. The *Odyssey*'s structure dramatizes a series of potential changes for the worse that can take place under the effect of time, movement, and absence, such changes as the possible bleaching of Odysseus' bones by the shores of the sounding sea, or his conceivable transformation in the course of his wanderings into the beggar he pretends to be, or the likelihood of his coming home to a ravaged home and a remarried wife. The comic structure of the *Odyssey* dramatizes the contingencies—including the contingent marvel of Odysseus' resiliency and wiliness—that block the seemingly inevitable changes.[21]

Odysseus, in his resiliency and suppleness, is typical of certain kinds of heroes, the heroes that stand at the center of the comedy of survival. Such heroes rise above circumstance by manipulating it even while accommodating to it. They are revealed to us in their canniness and keen consciousness of circumstance. They can remain themselves, unchanging, by virtue of their nimble responsiveness, a responsiveness that bends the world to their needs. In contrast to tragic victims, such as Shakespeare's Richard II, they can afford to waste both time and self. Richard II is dynamic, in my sense of the term, because he is at the center of a dynamic, wasting action, wholly subject to that action's corrosive effect because of his rigidity. Odysseus is flexible and static; because of his flexibility he is exempt from the corrosive effects of the *Odyssey*'s action.

Another kind of comic character is both static and rigid. I refer to such characters as Molière's miser and Jonson's Morose, who are rigid like Richard and are defeated like Richard because they lack the responsiveness, the malleability, and the resilient canniness of an Odysseus. *The Miser* and *The Silent Woman* are structured to render process, the process of works in the traditions of New Comedy, which, as Northrop Frye describes it, cast out the rigid blocking figures that are at their center. But the process is of (and in) the world, and not of the character. Harpagon and Morose are variously complex, but their complexity partakes of the static schematism of a Micawber; their rigidities bespeak kinship to him.

With Harpagon-like characters who stand statically at the center of a dynamic action we approach one of the extreme possibilities for the relationship between a character and its literary context. I refer to farcical actions, within which we have process, but process generated by harshly external and physical actions and events. In farce, characters far more mechanized than Micawber, and infinitely simplified, are bowled over by circumstances more mechanical and external than any a Micawber is involved in. Simplification and mechanization extend so far in farce that it is often hard to speak of schematism in character. This is because characters in farce have so few traits that they hardly form a paradigm and are utterly absorbed into the schematic reductionism of the action. To this extent, they too are, like figures in folktales and like the "narrative men" of *The Arabian Nights*, mere functions of the text in which they perform.

Yet narrative men are as abstractable from texts as the protagonists of Shakespeare's tragedies or Tolstoy's novels, and vice versa. The qualities of characters, as denizens of literary texts rather than as simulacra of people we might know, depend on the entire constellation of elements in the texts that generate them. Yet whatever their qualities, they hold the possibility of severance from their "living" (meaning their verbal) context. Sinbad the Sailor can be considered in and for himself as well as Anna Karenina can, and Hamlet can be contemplated "on his own" no less than the grotesques of the *Dunciad*.

How far we choose to abstract and autonomize them—to liberate them from the texts that are their life medium—depends, of course, on our critical bias and on the kind of reading that this bias dictates. My argument throughout has been that we can abstract them if we choose to and that the act of abstraction is a legitimate, though controlled, aspect of our relation to literature. Beyond that, a considerable number—if not the great majority—of literary texts demand that we abstract the characters from them in the course of analyzing them in order to grasp the implicit or explicit logic of their actions, their worlds, their thematic concerns. Even the very language of literature remains incomprehensible if we carry too far the view that characters of literature are not hes, shes, thems, but rather *its*. Reference of pronouns, in a work that generates characters, remains incomprehensible unless we posit—and abstract—the figment to which it refers, however ambiguously.

Afterword: On the Resolution
of Character into Text

Characters, of course, need not be abstracted from their texts or treated as relatively autonomous entities with some resemblance to people in life. Quite the contrary. Characters may and often must be resolved back into the text, and this may be done in many ways, including those briefly touched upon in chapter 1. Such resolution, tantamount at times to dissolution, of character into text can be thematic, imagistic, psychological, sociological, formal, or linguistic.

Whichever approach we choose, the resolution of characters into text involves reversing the procedures of abstracting them so that they become relatively autonomous. Such resolution and dissolution are sometimes difficult, especially for characters who, in a manner of speaking, invite us to confront them in their own right, as themselves. On the other hand, for characters whom we have to wrench and even warp in order to give them any semblance of autonomy, the process of resolution into text is rather simple. In *The Tempest*, Ceres, as goddess of plenty, must be rudely forced into independent existence; she subsides comfortably into the whole verbal and imagic context of *The Tempest*, where her function is to preside over a feast and to symbolize plenty. Anna Karenina, for her part, is a figure who boldly stands forth as herself, as "literally" herself, and she therefore resists such dissolution rather strongly. To dissolve her back into her text demands a wrenching almost as strong as the wrenching of Ceres when we choose to consider her maternal feelings.

Yet however salient Anna Karenina may be as a being in her own right, she can nonetheless be resolved back into the field of discourse that generates her. Even while we may see her as a vividly dramatized simulacrum of a person, we can also see her as a highly dramatized embodiment of a thematic tension, such as the tension between mechanism and organic life. *Anna Karenina* is concerned (and Lukács is eloquent on the subject) with the transition from an agrarian aristocratic society to a more urban, industrializing, capitalist one.[1] The symbols of this tension are horses of various sorts and railroads. But the process is directly articulated through people. Stiva, Anna's brother, moves in the course of the novel from old-fashioned, down-at-the-heels aristocratic wastrelhood to newfangled philandering on his income as a member of the Railroads Board. Anna herself moves from a shabby-genteel aristocratic childhood to her life as the wife of a bureaucratic functionary and then to her existence as the mistress of a man who runs an estate on the principles of mechanized British farming. It is not just Anna's riding clothes that are on the advanced British model. Even the birth control she practices is seen as part of a ratiocinative, scientific, mechanically egotistic tampering with nature. Seen from this point of view, Anna is broken on the wheel of Vronsky's progressive, self-involved abstraction from her and her needs, even as she is undermined by the mechanism of her narcissistic grief, which drives her to her death under the wheels of the iron horse.

Anna's development in the course of the novel, despite all of the feeling that accompanies it, can be seen (and from a certain vantage point must be seen) as a movement from luminous, organic life to mechanical drivenness. That movement, when we focus on it, diverts us from Anna as a suffering person and orients us to the way that her qualities are interwoven with other elements in the text. Hence her destruction becomes not a human catastrophe but part of a structure in which we consider her fate by light of analogy to other things, like the breaking of the back of Vronsky's horse Frou-Frou or the fluttering of birds to which Frou-Frou's death throes are compared. The horse's injury is caused by Vronsky's self-involved, mechanical failure to attune himself to the natural rhythm of the high-strung mare's movement. It is appropriate that at the novel's end we should see Vronsky in uniform, on a train, with a toothache, going to fight in an absurd, knee-jerk imperialist war. At the end, it is not Vronsky's particular character traits that matter but rather the configuration of mechanical images, situations, and settings within which we find him.

I find if difficult to reduce Anna, or even Vronsky, to an embodiment of traits and processes that enact these themes of mechanism and organicism; yet it seems to me possible to understand Anna at least partially in these terms. Indeed, if we are to grasp the novel as a whole in all its complexity, we must understand Anna in this way, at least provisionally, as one stage of our contemplation of her character. Contemplation of Anna in this perspective is elicited by the rich configuration of images—horse and iron horse, with their accompanying imagery of hammer and anvil, in the context of the little peasant for railroad and of flying birds for horse—that surround her. Such images are an integral part of the novel's texture as well as a vehicle for governing themes, and hence they are also a means of precipitating our image of the characters.

The configuration of images for Anna is rich, but not nearly so rich as it is for Catherine Earnshaw in *Wuthering Heights*. I deal with Anna at length because she is relatively difficult to resolve back into a pattern of themes or images. Catherine is easier to resolve because she is far more deeply embedded in the imagistic and thematic components of the novel that generates her, as I suggested in chapter 3, when I took Elizabeth Bennet, not Anna, as a contrast to Catherine.

Catherine is directly and unequivocally identified with thematic elements and with such images as trees and the branches
of trees. Any reading of her character or of *Wuthering Heights*
must engage this identification. The process of identification
begins at the very opening of the novel, long before we hear
of her, when Lockwood's explanation of that "significant
provincial expression" *wuthering* transforms wind-bent thorn
trees into alms-seeking humanoids. It extends through
Lockwood's dream, in which Catherine's icy hand turns out
to be the branch of a fir tree rubbing against the window, and
includes both young Catherine's direct identification with
trees in her vision of heaven, when she speaks of lying on a
bough in the breeze, and her indirect identification, as
implied in the scene where she climbs down a tree to escape
from the Heights, a scene reminiscent of one in which her
mother visits Heathcliff with the help of the same tree. Similarly, the identification of Heathcliff with his name, with the
moors that he and Catherine raced on when they were
children, with Penistone Crags, and with Catherine's equation of her love for him with "the rocks beneath," serves to
abrogate our sense of Heathcliff as a person. The rock and
moor images fuse with the images of him as an elemental
creature so that we come to conceive of him as a part of the
elements—of nature, in opposition to civilization. Both
Catherine and Heathcliff, by a process of displacement away
from their identity as human beings, come to be perceived as
the things they are compared to and as part of the pattern of
images that expresses a tension between wild nature and
effeminate or repressive civilization.

Again, to resolve either the characters in *Wuthering Heights*
or *Anna Karenina* into thematic patterns and patterns of
imagery is to reverse the procedures we perform when we
abstract the characters as elements in their own right. In the
latter process, we subordinate the images to the characters,
reading images as adjuncts to the characters' manifest traits
or as metaphors that convey aspects of their personalities. In
the former process, we subordinate the characters themselves

to such elements as imagery or thematic structures. Catherine and Heathcliff, in theme- or image-centered readings, are not tormented lovers whose identification with each other and whose wish to fuse with each other are enunciated in imagery of splitting trees and underlying masses of rock. Rather, they are elemental creatures who "become" the trees, the winds, and the rocks; they become the elements with which they also identify. Their existence as characters—as simulacra of people, within the limits defined by the text—becomes a part of the pattern that the novel uses them to create.

The polarization of possible ways of perceiving the work—whether to foreground the characters, as in children's pop-up books, and then abstract them and consider them in themselves, or, alternatively, to flatten them and see them as part of an overall design—involves an op-art set of shifting perspectives, of focusing and refocusing perception. In opera we may see (or hear) arias (or even recitatives) as part of a dramatic structure involving characters, and therefore processes of characterization, in the development of musical as well as verbal and dramatic elements. Alternatively, we may apprehend the verbal elements (arias and recitatives) as part of a "pure" musical structure in which differentiated vocal patterns are assimilated into the pattern of the music as a whole. Analogously, in perceiving paintings we experience a tension between the patterns of visualization (the "subject") of a painting and the formal, compositional, painterly elements organized within the whole. In literature, as in opera or painting, we rarely experience a work wholly in terms of either polarized possibility; rather we synthesize the two along the way. But the option of perceiving the work and its elements in either perspective remains, whether for the sake of understanding or for pleasure.

Characters can also be resolved into other elements in the text. They can, for example, be resolved back into the psychological elements that animate not *them* as the simulacra of possible people but rather the *texts* that generate them. And they can be resolved back into the psychological dimensions of the text in a number of ways. If we think of the text as the dynamic but stabilized fantasy of the author, we will ask what the characters symbolize in the author's imagination. We might think of Catherine as a projection of Brontë's wishes, for example, and of Heathcliff as Brontë's demon lover.[2] Or we might think of both of them as ciphers in a more primitive fantasy of fusion with a lost or absent mother. Alternatively, we can think of the text as separate from its author and conceive of it as embodying an autonomous fantasy that constellates around a central figure. In that case, it is the central figure's conflicts that are projected into the other characters through all the language and situations in the novel. If we see Heathcliff as central, Heathcliff becomes the abandoned child, whose trajectory involves violent rage at the loss of its mother and a series of maneuvers, first to compensate for the loss by fusing with Catherine or with symbols of Catherine and then to avenge himself on those who prevent such fusion.[3] If we see the novel in this light, we retain Heathcliff as a character and reduce everyone else to a function of his inner system of symbolization. In such a reading, however, he too is reduced from the figure we retrieve from the surface of his presentation to a relatively schematic patterning of his presumed wishes. The difference between the manifest Heathcliff and the X-ray patterning of his psychic entrails is the difference between, say, Freud's Wolf Man as he emerges from his own memoir and the Wolf Man we know from Freud's case history.[4] The crucial point, though, is that whether we see Catherine as a correlative of Heathcliff or see both Heathcliff and Catherine as ciphers in a fantasy that we attribute to Brontë, we are thinking of them not as themselves but as symbols in a pattern that resolves them into elements or functions of the system of fantasy in the novel.

What we can do in psychological terms we can do in sociohistorical terms as well, though here the reduction will probably be less total. If we think of Heathcliff, for example, as a projection of the condition of the working class in

England in 1847, we may react to him in terms of what we feel about his social situation. This is so even in a moderately Marxist reading such as Arnold Kettle's, in which we are asked to see Heathcliff as himself but also to sympathize with him and his dehumanizing brutality on the basis of our understanding of what he might have suffered as one of the insulted and injured in Victorian society.[5] Marx and Engels read Balzac still more radically in this way, and so do Lukács and Fredric Jameson. Père Goriot is to be seen not as himself but as the epitome of a condition; Gobseck is not himself but a meeting point or battleground for contradictions in a historical moment.[6] Here the allegorization is extreme and involves displacement of the emphasis from the apprehension of characters as literally themselves to apprehension of them as symbolic of something else. For Brontë and Balzac it involves such displacement in texts that would seem to ask us to contemplate characters, much of the time, as literally themselves. Lukács directly and deliberately confronts this issue in speaking of literature as containing human types that epitomize intellectual or moral response, a kind of "ideal type," if I may borrow Max Weber's category. Whatever terminology we apply to the procedure, it is clear that Marxist treatments of character involve the reading of textual elements as parables of historical process.

Sociohistorical reductions need not be Marxist, of course. John Danby reads *King Lear* as an account of the conflict involved in the transition from Christian-feudal values to capitalist ones. Danby sees the characters in the play, or rather the polarized groups of characters, as representing typical social and moral attitudes. Such attitudes, in his account, not only epitomize the characters but effectively exhaust them.[7] Not far from Danby's historical reading of Shakespeare are those of Theodore Spencer and a goodly number of other Christianizing moralists. The New Critical readings, with their moral and thematic emphases (which I touched on in chapter 1), are also closely related to them.

As for formal reductions, the whole range of readings that

stress the "realistic" and "artistic" motivation mentioned in chapter 1 rather than psychological motivation belong to this class. A psychological reading of *Great Expectations* takes Magwitch to signify Pip's guilt, externalized. Such a reading may orient the guilt to Pip himself as a character, or it may subordinate the literal Pip to the pattern of guilt-inducing and guilt-vanquishing strategies that the novel depicts.[8] A formal reading dispenses with both the literal Pip and the literal Magwitch and sees Magwitch as an instrument for the advancement of the plot. The plot requires a benefactor who is not Miss Havisham, and that benefactor has to be one who will shame Pip into consciousness of his expectations and their falsity and one who will also serve to explicate the Pip–Estella connection in the grand denouement of the action. Analogously, in such a reading we have not only Magwitch as the facilitator of events but also Pip as presenter of events. Thus the first-person Pip narrative is not a means of revealing Pip but a means of projecting the images of all the other figures and the action as a whole. Pip himself, therefore, need not be confronted as a motivated entity, or indeed as a character at all.

The possibilities of such reductions are endless. A brilliant deconstructionist reading of *The Ambassadors* sidesteps Strether as a character and reads him as a means of dramatizing the mediated nature of all communication. In such a reading the focus of the novel is not Strether's human dilemma, his tormented choice between Woollet and Paris, but rather his function as a "representative" who must represent Woollet to Paris and then Paris to Woollet, with all the difficulties that such representation entails, including the difficulties of language itself as the medium of representation.[9] The thrust of such a reading is to reduce all the characters to ciphers in a drama of language and communication—a legitimate drama, which is there in the text, but which tends to overwhelm the characters or to bleed them of their illusion of substance.

The farthest-reaching of such character-dissolving approaches is, as I noted in my first chapter, the semiotic approach, which strives to reduce characters to their verbal and grammatical components. I myself find such readings almost incomprehensible, but it seems to me that they are in principle legitimate. What they do is reduce the characters to lexical and grammatical components of the verbal composition of the text, and then, if the reader chooses to do so, read them in terms of patterns in the text other than character-generating ones. Such patterns, as Joel Weinsheimer suggests in his reading of *Emma*, may be thematic or formal.[10] They exclude sociological or simple psychological readings, however, because such readings tend to start from the surface structure of a story, the structure in which characters self-evidently figure. In a radically linguistic approach, the neutralization of characters even as provisional entities obviates a reading that starts from the surface, the appearance, of the character as him or herself—a surface that less fundamentalist approaches confront, if only in order to dissolve it.

But there is no point in laboring the full range of possibilities for absorbing characters back into their generating texts. My point here is merely that such absorptions back into text are possible, legitimate, and often desirable. Indeed, any consideration of character in itself, such as the one I have attempted in this study, must take them into account. But to limit our consideration of character to such procedures is to forgo character altogether as a source of pleasure and an object of contemplation. That is an eventuality that I, for one, am not willing to entertain, not only because it involves renouncing the pleasures of communing with characters, but because much of what matters most in literature can be tapped only through them. It is not only that, by my lights, we seem "naturally" to envision and to extrapolate characters from texts, but that we *should* do so if we are to apprehend those texts in the richest way possible.

Notes

Chapter 1. The Case against Character

1. On the achievement of the moderns in character creation, see Baruch Hochman, *The Test of Character: From the Victorian Novel to the Modern* (Rutherford, N.J., 1983), esp. pp. 207–212.

2. See, among others, Bell Gale Chevigny's introduction to *Twentieth-Century Interpretations: Endgame* (Englewood Cliffs, N.J., 1969); J. E. Dearlove, *Accommodating to Chaos: Samuel Beckett's Nonrelational Art* (Durham, N.C., 1982), esp. chap. 3.

3. The view is epidemic. See, among others, Alain Robbe-Grillet, *For a New Novel*, trans. Richard Howard (New York, 1965), pp. 25–29; José Ortega y Gasset, *The Dehumanization of Art; and Notes on the Novel* (Princeton, 1948), pp. 9–10, 90–96; Tony Tanner, introduction to *City of Words: American Fiction, 1950–70* (London, 1971), pp. 15–31.

4. W. John Harvey, *Character and the Novel* (Ithaca, 1965), pp. 191–212.

5. Roland Barthes, *S/Z*, trans. Richard Miller (New York, 1974), p. 95; Jonathan Culler, *Structuralist Poetics* (Ithaca, 1975), pp. 230–233; Everett Knight, *Theory of the Classical Novel* (London, 1970), chap. 1.

6. E. E. Stoll, *Art and Artifice in Shakespeare* (New York, 1951); Bruno Snell, *The Discovery of the Mind*, trans. T. G. Rosenmeyer (New York, 1960), chap. 1.

7. G. Wilson Knight, *The Wheel of Fire* (London, 1961), pp. 9–12.

8. Ibid.

9. L. C. Knights, "How Many Children Had Lady Macbeth?" in *Explorations* (London, 1965), pp. 1–39.

10. Samuel Butler, *Notebooks*, quoted on title page of Claude C. H. Williamson, ed., *Readings on the Character of Hamlet* (1974).

11. Ernest Jones, *Hamlet and Oedipus* (New York, 1952), pp. 20, 22.

12. A. C. Bradley, *Shakespearean Tragedy* (Greenwich, Conn., n.d.), pp. 19–20, 26–29. Originally published in 1904.

13. T. S. Eliot, "Tradition and the Individual Talent," in *Selected Essays* (New York, 1950), pp. 3–11.

14. C. H. Rickword, "A Note on Fiction," in F. R. Leavis, ed., *Toward a Standard of Criticism* (London, 1931), reprinted in Roger Sale, ed., *Discussions of the Novel* (Boston, 1960), p. 79.

15. Ibid., pp. 80–81.

16. O. B. Hardison, in O. B. Hardison and H. Golden, eds., *Aristotle's Poetics* (Englewood Cliffs, N.J., 1968), p. 122, cited in Seymour Chatman, *Story and Discourse* (Ithaca, 1978), p. 117.

17. Martin Price, "The Other Self: Thoughts about Character in the Novel," in Maynard Mack and Ian Gregor, eds., *Imagined Worlds* (London 1968), pp. 292–293.

18. Rawdon Wilson, "On Character: A Reply to Martin Price," *Critical Inquiry* 2 (Autumn 1975): 194.

19. Rawdon Wilson, "The Bright Chimera: Character as a Literary Term," *Critical Inquiry* 5 (1979): 735–737.

20. Monroe Beardsley, *Aesthetics: Problems in the Philosophy of Criticism* (New York, 1958), p. 403.

21. G. Wilson Knight, "An Essay on *Hamlet*," in *Wheel of Fire*, pp. 23–42.

22. Vladimir Propp, *Morphology of the Folk Tale* (Austin, 1977).

23. See p. 15.

24. Henry James, *The Art of Fiction* (New York, 1948), p. 13.

25. Henry James, Preface to *The Portrait of a Lady* (Harmondsworth, 1960), p. x.

26. Bradley, *Shakespearean Tragedy*, pp. 184–196; Leo Tolstoy, "Shakespeare and the Drama," in *Recollections and Essays*, trans. Aylmer Maude (London, 1937), pp. 307, 383, 336, 351; William Archer, *The Old Drama and the New* (London, 1923), pp. 39–49.

27. Boris Tomashevsky, "Thematics," in Lee T. Lemon and Marion J. Reis, eds., *Russian Formalist Criticism: Four Essays* (Lincoln, Neb., 1965), pp. 78–87; Ladislav Matejka and Krystyna Pomorska, eds., *Readings in Russian Poetics: Formalist and Structuralist Views* (Cambridge, Mass., 1971), pp. 18–20.

28. Roland Barthes, "Introduction à l'analyse structurale des récits," *Communications* 8 (1966): 1–27, published in English as "Introduction to the Structural Analysis of Texts," trans. Lionel Duisit, in *New Literary History* 5 (1975), pp. 237–272; Tzvetan Todorov, *Grammaire du "Décameron"* (The Hague, 1969), pp. 27–30; Barthes, *S/Z*, p. 17. The breach opened by Barthes in *S/Z* was stormed by Seymour Chatman in *Story and Discourse* (Ithaca, 1978), pp. 113–126.

29. Gérard Genette, "Vraisemblance et motivation," *Communications* 11 (1969): 21–22.

30. Tzvetan Todorov, "Narrative Men," in *The Poetics of Prose*, trans. Richard Howard (Ithaca, 1977), pp. 66–69.

31. Algirdas Julien Greimas, *Semantique structurale* (Paris, 1966); Claude Bremond, *Logique du récit* (Paris, 1973).

32. See, for example, Gerald Prince, *A Grammar of Stories* (The Hague, 1973).

33. Joel Weinsheimer, "Theory of Character: *Emma*," *Poetics Today* 1 (Autumn 1979): 185–211.

34. Leo Bersani, *A Future for Astyanax: Character and Desire in Literature* (Boston, 1976); Hélène Cixous, "The Character of 'Character,'" *New Literary History* 5 (1974): 383–402.

35. On Cervantes, see Robert Alter, *Partial Magic* (Berkeley, 1975), chap. 1; Angel Flores, *Cervantes across the Centuries* (New York: Gordian Press, 1948); for Sterne, see Violet Khazoum, "The Inverted Comedy of *Tristram Shandy*," *Hebrew University Studies in Literature* 7 (Autumn 1979): 139–160.

36. Vladimir Nabokov, *The Real Life of Sebastian Knight* (Norfolk, Conn., 1941).

Chapter 2. On the Reality of Character in Literature

1. Kenneth A. Telford, *Aristotle's Poetics: Translation and Analysis* (Chicago, 1961), chap. 13, pp. 23–25, and chap. 15, pp. 27–29.

2. See Irma Brandeis, *The Ladder of Vision: A Study of Dante's "Comedy"* (Garden City, N.Y., 1962), pp. 19–26.

3. Thomas Rymer, *Critical Works*, ed. C. A. Zimansky (New Haven, 1956), pp. 131–164.

4. Maurice Morgann, *An Essay on the Dramatic Character of Falstaff* (1777), excerpted in G. K. Hunter, ed., *Casebook on Henry IV, Parts 1 and 2* (New York, 1970), pp. 25–55.

5. See chap. 1, n. 26.

6. Ian Watt surveys some of the presuppositions in *The Rise of the Novel* (Berkeley, 1967), pp. 9–30.

7. For Homer, see Albert B. Lord's survey of the issue in *The Singer of Tales* (New York, 1973), pp. 158–197; for the Bible, see Robert Alter, *The Art of Biblical Narrative* (New York, 1981); for Shakespeare, John Dover Wilson formulates the issues in *What Happened in Hamlet* (Cambridge, England, 1967).

8. Edward Bullough is perhaps the best-known academic affirmer of distance; see Bullough, *Aesthetics: Lectures and Essays* (London, 1957). Freud, of course, affirms the antithetical close-involvement view, which has deep roots in the tradition, extending back to Aristotle; see, among other essays, "The Relation of the Poet to Day Dreaming," reprinted in Sigmund Freud, *Character and Culture*, ed. Phillip Rieff (New York, 1963). The essay was first published in 1908.

9. From here in on I will refer chiefly to verbal constructs—i.e., literary works—but what I have to say is transposable to other media.

10. Rawdon Wilson, "The Bright Chimera: Character as a Literary Term," *Critical Inquiry* 5 (1979): 533–535.

11. See especially Roman Ingarden, *The Literary Work of Art*, trans. George C. Grabowicz (Evanston, Ill., 1973), esp. pp. 250–254 and 331–355; Wolfgang Iser, *The Act of Reading* (London, 1978), esp. pp. 170–231, and "Indeterminacy in the Reader's Response in Prose Fiction," in J. Hillis Miller, ed., *Aspects of Narrative: Selected Papers from the English Institute* (New York, 1971), pp. 1–46.

12. Seymour Chatman, *Story and Discourse* (Ithaca, 1978), chap. 3, pp. 96–145; W. John Harvey, *Character and the Novel* (Ithaca, 1965).

13. Chatman, *Story and Discourse*, pp. 118–119. See also Jonathan Culler, *Flaubert* (Ithaca, 1974), pp. 89.

14. Chatman, *Story and Discourse*, pp. 119–127, 118.

15. Ibid., pp. 118, 119–123.

16. Ibid., pp. 128–130.

17. Yosef Ewen, *Character in Narrative* (in Hebrew), (Tel Aviv, 1980), pp. 49, 56, 99–124.

18. Howard Michael Felperin, *Shakespearean Representation: Mimesis and Modernity in Elizabethan Tragedy* (Princeton, 1977), pp. 7–9.

19. Harvey, *Character and the Novel*, pp. 54, 73, 111.

20. Ibid., p. 54.

21. Ibid., p. 110.

22. The best account I know of how character is reconstructed from a text is to be found in Shlomith Rimmon-Kenan, *Narrative Fiction* (London, 1983), pp. 36–40.

23. For sharp formulation of the problem, see Norman N. Holland, *Poems in Persons* (New York, 1975), pp. 68–100, and *5 Readers Reading* (New Haven, 1977).

24. For an overview of the reader-oriented approaches, see Susan R. Suleiman, "Varieties of Audience-Oriented Criticism," introduction to S. R. Suleiman and I. Crosman, eds., *The Reader in the Text: Essays on Audience and Interpretation* (Princeton, 1980), pp. 3–45.

25. Harvey, *Character and the Novel*, p. 31.

26. E. M. Forster, *Aspects of the Novel* (New York, 1927), pp. 103–118.

27. Harvey, *Character and the Novel*, pp. 56–59.

28. Mary McCarthy, "Character in Fiction," *Partisan Review* 28 (1961): 172–174; John Bayley, *The Character of Love: A Study in the Literature of Personality* (New York, 1963), pp. 37–38.

29. G. H. Mead, *Mind, Self, Society* (Chicago, 1934); Jacques Lacan, *Écrits I* (Paris, 1966).

30. Bayley, *Character of Love*, p. 36.

31. Northrop Frye, *Anatomy of Criticism* (Princeton, 1957), pp. 171–172.

32. Georg Lukács, *Studies in European Realism* (New York, 1964), pp. 6–8.

33. Nicholas Wolterstorff, "Characters and Their Names," *Poetics* 8 (1979): 101–127, is illuminating on the issue of types and "kinds" in talking about characters.

34. Virginia Woolf, "Character in Fiction," *Criterion* 2 (July 1924).

35. John Romano, *Dickens and Reality* (New York, 1978), esp. pp. 5–7 and 50–82.

36. Freud's view of character as a structure of defense against instinctual conflict and Reich's analogous view of rigidity and body

armor bear directly on the conceptualization of such characters. See Sigmund Freud, "Character and Anal Erotism," in Sigmund Freud, *Character and Culture*, ed. Phillip Rieff (New York, 1963), and Wilhelm Reich, *Character Analysis*, 3d ed., trans. Vincent E. Carafagno (New York, 1972). For discussion of these issues see chaps. 4 and 5.

37. See Moshe Ron, "Autobiographical Narration and Formal Closure in *Great Expectations*," *Hebrew University Studies in Literature* 5 (Spring 1977); Shlomith Rimmon, *The Concept of Ambiguity: The Example of Henry James* (Chicago, 1977), pp. 116–166.

38. John Keats, "On Sitting Down to Read *King Lear* Once Again."

39. The radical Freudian view is best formulated by Wilhelm Reich in *Character Analysis*.

40. Wilson, "Bright Chimera," p. 747.

41. For an extreme instance of such reduction, see John Rutherford, "Galdós's 'El amigo manso,'" in Roger Fowler, ed., *Style and Structure in Literature: Essays in the New Stylistics* (Ithaca, 1975), pp. 177–211, and John O'Toole, "Approaches to Narrative Structure," in ibid., pp. 143–176.

42. Think, for example, of Mr. Micawber and his various oral fixations. (For a discussion, see chap. 5.)

43. For Lukács' view of characters, see his *Studies in European Realism* and *Theory of the Novel* (Cambridge, Mass., 1972); for Jameson, see his *Political Unconscious: Narrative as a Socially Symbolic Act* (Ithaca, 1982).

44. Richard A. Lanham, *Motives of Eloquence* (New Haven, 1976), p. 60.

45. Aristotle, *The Ethics of Aristotle: The Nicomachean Ethics*, trans. J. A. K. Thomson (Harmondsworth, 1956), bk. II, pp. 55–75.

46. Clifford Geertz has done vital work in this area. See his *Interpretation of Cultures* (New York, 1973). In literary studies, Stephen Greenblatt's *Renaissance Self-Fashioning: From More to Shakespeare* (Chicago, 1980), and Arnold Weinstein's *Fictions of the Self: 1550–1800* (Princeton, 1981) take on a piece of the job.

47. See, e.g., Vladimir Nabokov, *Lolita* (New York, 1966), pp. 7, 34.

Chapter 3. Homo Fictus, Homo Sapiens

1. Meredith Anne Skura, *The Literary Use of the Psychoanalytic Process* (New Haven, 1981), pp. 38–57.

2. David Hume, *A Treatise of Human Nature*, ed. D. G. C. Macnabb (London, n.d.), pt. 3, sec. 6, pp. 300–312; Amelie Oxenhandler Rorty, ed., *The Identities of Persons* (Berkeley, 1976).

3. Jonathan Culler, *Flaubert* (Ithaca, 1974), pp. 89–90.

4. E. M. Forster, *Aspects of the Novel* (New York, 1927), pp. 87, 99.

5. See Marcel Proust, *Swann's Way*, trans. C. K. Scott-Moncrieff (New York, 1970), pp. 64–65.

6. Rawdon Wilson, "The Bright Chimera: Character as a Literary Term," *Critical Inquiry* 5 (1979): 747.

7. Rawdon Wilson, "On Character: A Reply to Martin Price," *Critical Inquiry* 2 (1975): 195.

8. Janet Adelman, Introduction to *Twentieth-Century Interpretations of "King Lear"* (Englewood Cliffs, N.J., 1978), pp. 1–21.

9. See, again, the studies by Rutherford and O'Toole (chap. 2, n. 41) for thematic analysis. Such studies as Janet Adelman's of *King Lear* (cited in n. 8, above) and Meir Sternberg's of a series of works (e.g., *Odyssey, Pride and Prejudice, The Ambassadors*) richly exemplify the phenomenon. See Meir Sternberg, *Expositional Modes and Temporal Ordering* (Baltimore, 1978).

10. See W. John Harvey, *Character and the Novel* (Ithaca, 1965), pp. 32, 52–60, 69.

11. Martin Price, "The Irrelevant Detail and the Emergence of Form," in J. Hillis Miller, ed., *Aspects of Narrative: Selected Papers from the English Institute* (New York, 1971).

12. William H. Gass, *Fiction and the Figures of Life* (New York, 1970), p. 60.

13. Case histories and diaries or memoirs exemplify the phenomenon in the extreme. See, for an exemplary case, Muriel Gardiner, ed., *The Wolf Man by The Wolf Man* (New York, 1971), with its juxtaposition of Freud's case history and the Wolf Man's own memoir.

14. For an anatomy of the term, see Francis Fergusson, *Dante* (New York, 1966).

15. Baruch Hochman, "Joyce's *Portrait* as Portrait," *Literary Review* 22 (Fall 1978): 32–42.

16. The best available account in English of the verbal and formal means of presenting consciousness in fiction is to be found in Dorrit Cohn, *Transparent Minds* (Princeton, 1978). I have avoided a more extensive account of the issues Cohn deals with because it seems to me that although preoccupation with consciousness in the novel reflects an interest in character, there is no necessary correlation between the extensive representation of consciousness and the effective projection of character.

17. Antoinette B. Dauber, "Allegory and Irony in *Othello*," unpublished essay.

18. Northrop Frye, *Anatomy of Criticism* (Princeton, 1957), pp. 304–305.

19. Ibid., p. 305.

20. See my chapter "*Wuthering Heights:* Unity and Scope, Surface and Depth," in *The Test of Character: From the Victorian Novel to the Modern* (Rutherford, N.J., 1983), and Dorothy Van Ghent, *The English Novel: Form and Function*, pp. 153–170.

21. Otto Rank, *The Double: A Psychoanalytic Study*, trans. Harry Tucker, Jr., (Chapel Hill, 1971).

22. Forster, *Aspects of the Novel*, pp. 142–144.

23. See Leona Toker, "A Nabokovian Character in Conrad's *Nostromo*," *Revue de littérature comparée*. Forthcoming.

24. See Zvi Jagendorf, "All against One in *Troilus and Cressida*," *English* 141 (Autumn 1982): 199–210, and Elizabeth Freund, "Arachne's Broken Web," in Patricia Parker and Geoffrey Hartman, eds., *Shakespeare and the Question of Theory* (London, 1985).

25. See chap. 1, n. 30.

26. Bruno Bettelheim, *The Uses of Enchantment: The Meaning and Importance of Fairy Tales* (New York, 1977), pp. 266–270.

27. Joel Kovel, "On Reading *Madame Bovary* Psychoanalytically," *Seminars in Psychiatry* 4 (August 1973): 331–345.

28. Harold Bloom, *The Anxiety of Influence* (New York, 1973).

29. For mixing of modes in the nineteenth-century novel, see Robert Scholes and Robert Kellogg, *The Nature of Narrative* (New York, 1968), pp. 230–231, and Donald Fanger, *Dostoevsky and Romantic Realism* (Chicago, 1967), pp. 3–27.

30. See Shimon Sandbank, "Myth and Anti-myth in Kafka" (in Hebrew), in *Kafka Symposium* (Tel Aviv: Sifriyat Hapoalim, 1982), pp. 44–45.

Chapter 4. Characters in Their Kinds: A Taxonomy

1. W. John Harvey, *Character and the Novel* (Ithaca, 1965), pp. 52–55.

2. Ibid., pp. 56–58.

3. Henry James, Preface to *The Portrait of a Lady* (Harmondsworth, 1960), p. xv.

4. Harvey, *Character and the Novel*, p. 56.

5. Yosef Ewen proposes three scales for categorizing character: a scale of development, of complexity, and of verisimilitude. See *Character in Narrative* (Tel Aviv, 1980), pp. 34–44. It seems to me that a more complex grid of qualities is needed for encompassing character in literature and for acknowledging the complexity of a phenomenon requiring even the limited cumbersomeness of Ewen's categories.

6. E. H. Gombrich, "Meditations on a Hobby Horse, or the Roots of Artistic Form," in *Meditations on a Hobby Horse* (London, 1978), pp. 1–11.

7. See J. Leeds Barroll, *The Formation of Character in the Tragedies of Shakespeare* (Columbia, S.C., 1974), pp. 65, 70, 225.

8. Northrop Frye, *Anatomy of Criticism* (Princeton, 1957), pp. 33–35.

9. For treatment of such division of characters in the novel, see H. M. Daleski, *The Divided Heroine: A Recurrent Pattern in Six English Novels* (New York, 1984).

10. Ian Watt, *The Rise of the Novel* (Berkeley, 1967), pp. 93–134.

11. Dorothy Van Ghent, *The English Novel: Form and Function* (New York, 1953), pp. 33–43.

12. I use the term *formal realism* in Ian Watt's sense. See *Rise of the Novel*, pp. 9–34.

13. Harvey sums up the problem in the appendix, "The Retreat from Character," to his *Character and the Novel*, esp. pp. 201–205.

14. See, for example, Leon Edel's summary of the challenge to the biographer: *Literary Biography* (London, 1957).

15. George Santayana, *Three Philosophical Poets* (New York, 1970), pp. 130–179.

16. Forster, *Aspects of the Novel* (New York, 1927), pp. 102–103; Edwin Muir, *The Structure of the Novel* (London, 1974), pp. 62ff.

17. Harvey, *Character and the Novel*, pp. 73–110.

18. Clearly, there is a possibility of "taking" a figure like the Fool

as a "whole" person—of envisioning the tremulously clinging, fiercely assertive qualities of his performance and elaborating them into a type of prematurely, precociously, incisive, childlike identity in an adult who behaves as the Fool does. But such elaboration is the sort that constructs an image of what "this *kind* of person would do" rather than of what this particular person is. See Nicholas Wolterstorff, "Worlds of Works of Art," *Journal of Aesthetics and Art History* 35 (Winter 1976): 128–129.

19. Chatman classifies "flat"—fragmentary, or incomplete— characters as "teleological" and "round" ones as "agglomerative." See *Story and Discourse* (Ithaca, 1978), p. 132. I differ with him not in terminology but substantively. It is largely the purposive meaningfulness—the "teleology"—of a text that generates the sense of the wholeness and dimensionality of characters. Complex and dynamic characters are as "teleological" as their opposites. It is just that they engage us differently—that, as Chatman says, there is something "in" them that seems to be "left over."

20. Erich Auerbach, *Mimesis: The Representation of Reality in Western Literature*, trans. Willard Trask (Garden City, N.Y., n.d.), pp. 151–177.

21. Roman Jakobson, "The Metaphoric and Metonymic Poles," in Hazard Adams, ed., *Critical Theory since Plato* (New York, 1971), p. 1115.

22. See Murray Krieger, *Poetic Presence and Illusion* (Baltimore, 1979), p. 193.

23. Among others, John Jones, *On Aristotle and Greek Tragedy* (London, 1962), takes a position very different from my own, insisting on the plot-centeredness of Greek tragedy, as Aristotle saw it, and on the instrumentality of Oedipus within the plot of *Oedipus.*

24. Jane Austen, *Pride and Prejudice*, ed. Tony Tanner (Harmondsworth, 1975), p. 88. Elizabeth's terms are "deep and intricate" vs. their opposites.

25. Frye, *Anatomy of Criticism*, p. 44.

26. See Dorothea Krook, *The Ordeal of Consciousness in Henry James* (Cambridge, England, 1967), pp. 52–54.

27. Meir Sternberg, *Expositional Modes and Temporal Ordering* (Baltimore, 1978), p. 239.

28. J. I. M. Stewart, *Character and Motive in Shakespeare* (London, 1966), pp. 7–10, 30–39.

29. This point is pivotal in Harvey's view of fiction. He writes that "a surplus margin of gratuitous life, a sheer excess of material, a fecundity of detail and invention, a delighted submergence in experience, . . . all these are observable in the work of the great novelists" (*Character and the Novel*, p. 189). He cites Robert Langbaum *The Poetry of Experience* (London, 1952), pp. 223–224: "We mean by character just the element in excess of plot requirements, the element we call *individual* because it eludes and defies classification. The paradoxical defiance of classification does not so much describe the individual element by creating a new, more refined category, as it alludes symbolically to its ultimately enigmatic nature."

30. Mary McCarthy, "Characters in Fiction," *Partisan Review* 28 (1961): 172–174.

31. See chap. 3, n. 8.

32. Joseph H. Gardner, "Dickens, Romance and *McTeague*: A Study in Mutual Interpretation," *Essays in Literature* 1 (Spring 1974): 363–366.

33. Bruno Bettelheim, *The Uses of Enchantment: The Meaning and Importance of Fairy Tales* (New York, 1977), pp. 159–165.

34. See chap. 3, pp. 81–82.

Chapter 5. Kinds of Character, Kinds of Texts

1. E. M. Forster, *Aspects of the Novel* (New York, 1927), p. 130.

2. Edwin Muir, *Structure of the Novel* (London, 1974), pp. 62–63.

3. Ibid., p. 64.

4. See Joseph Frank, *The Widening Gyre: Crisis and Mastery in Modern Literature* (Bloomington, 1973), pp. 3–62.

5. The contrast between tragedy and comedy—Sophoclean vs. Aristophanic or even Shakespearean (e.g., *King Lear* vs. *As You Like It*)—easily exemplifies the qualities of centrality of character to action and manifest coherence of action. Aristotle's account of types of recognition (Kenneth A. Telford, *Aristotle's Poetics: Translation and Analysis* [Chicago, 1961], chap. 16, pars. 1454b11.19–24, pp. 30–32), implies such a relationship between elements.

6. On the picaresque, see Muir, *Structure of the Novel*, pp. 28–32.

7. Ruth Nevo, *Tragic Form in Shakespeare* (Princeton, 1972), esp. pp. 22–29.

8. Muir, *Structure of the Novel*, pp. 59–60.

9. Telford, *Aristotle's Poetics*, chap. 4, pars. 1449a11.8–19, p. 9.

10. Ibid., chap. 10, pars. 1452a12, pp. 19–20.

11. Ibid., chap. 11, pars. 1455b11.24, pp. 33–35; chap. 10, pars. 1452a11.30–34, p. 20.

12. Francis Fergusson, *The Idea of a Theatre* (Garden City, N.Y., 1953), pp. 30–31.

13. For treatment of gaps as a functional element of narrative, see Meir Sternberg and Menakhem Perry, "The King through Ironic Eyes: The Narrator's Devices in the Biblical Story of David and Bathsheba and Two Excursuses on the Theory of Narrative Texts," *HaSifrut* 1:263–292 (in Hebrew), esp. pp. 263–265; and Shlomith Rimmon, *The Concept of Ambiguity: The Case of Henry James* (Chicago, 1977), pp. 45–50.

14. Such image structures are widely analyzed, as in Norman N. Holland's "Fantasy and Defense in Faulkner's 'A Rose for Emily,'" *Hartford Studies in Literature* 4 (1972): 1–35, and Menakhem Perry, "Literary Dynamics: How the Order of a Text Creates Its Meanings (with an Analysis of Faulkner's 'A Rose for Emily')" *Poetics Today* 1 (Autumn 1979): 35–64, 311–361.

15. See Gérard Genette, *Narrative Discourse*, trans. Jane E. Lewin, (Ithaca, 1980).

16. Martha Graham's dance-drama *Klytemnestra* is interesting in this regard. It transposes scenes "narrated" by various actors (including the Chorus) into acted ones that are presented as externalizations of what goes on in its characters' consciousness.

17. Percy Lubbock, *The Craft of Fiction* (New York, 1947), pp. 1–2.

18. Virginia Woolf, "David Copperfield," *The Nation*, August 22, 1925, reprinted in Stephen Wall, ed., *Charles Dickens: A Critical Anthology* (Harmondsworth, 1970), p. 274.

19. See E. Pearlman, "David Copperfield's Dream of Drowning," in Leonard Tennenhouse, ed., *The Practice of Psychoanalytic Criticism* (Detroit, 1976), pp. 105–117.

20. Meir Sternberg, *Expositional Modes and Temporal Ordering* (Baltimore, 1978), p. 128.

21. See my essay "Joyce's *Ulysses* and Homer's *Odyssey*," *Scripta Hierosolymitana* 25 (1973): 214–219.

Afterword: On the Resolution of Character into Text

1. Georg Lukács, *Studies in European Realism* (New York, 1964), pp. 163–166.

2. See, among others, Richard Chase, "The Brontës, or Myth Domesticated," *Kenyon Review* 9 (1947): 487–506; and Thomas Moser, "What's the Matter with Emily Jane?" in Moser, ed., *Wuthering Heights: Texts, Sources, Critics* (New York, 1962).

3. Joel Kovel, "Heathcliff's Quest," *Hebrew University Studies in Literature* 13 (Spring 1985).
Modern (Rutherford, N.J., 1983), pp. 106–109.

4. Sigmund Freud, "The Wolf Man," in Muriel Gardiner, ed., *The Wolf Man by The Wolf Man* (New York, 1971).

5. Arnold Kettle, *An Introduction to the English Novel*, vol. 1, *Defoe to George Eliot* (New York, 1965), pp. 139–155.

6. Lukács, *Studies in European Realism*, pp. 10–14; Fredric Jameson, *The Political Unconscious: Narrative as a Socially Symbolic Act* (Ithaca, 1982), pp. 151–184.

7. John Danby, *Shakespeare's Doctrine of Nature* (London, 1962).

8. Dorothy Van Ghent, *The English Novel: Form and Function* (New York, 1953), pp. 129–138.

9. John Landau, "*The Ambassadors: The Story of the Story*," *Hebrew University Studies in Literature* 12 (Spring 1984): 85–115.

10. Joel Weinsheimer, "Theory of Character: *Emma*," *Poetics Today* 1 (Autumn 1979): 185–201.

Bibliography

Adelman, Janet, ed. Introduction to *Twentieth-Century Interpretations of "King Lear."* Englewood Cliffs, N.J.: Prentice-Hall, 1978.

Alter, Robert. *The Art of Biblical Narrative.* New York: Basic Books, 1981.

——. *Partial Magic.* Berkeley: University of California Press, 1975.

Archer, William. *The Old Drama and the New.* London: William Heinemann, 1923.

Aristotle. *The Ethics of Aristotle: The Nicomachean Ethics.* Trans. J. A. K. Thomson. Harmondsworth: Penguin, 1956.

Auerbach, Erich. *Mimesis: The Representation of Reality in Western Literature.* Trans. Willard Trask. Garden City, N.Y.: Doubleday Anchor, n.d.

Barroll, J. Leeds. *The Formation of Character in the Tragedies of Shakespeare.* Columbia: University of South Carolina Press, 1974.

Barthes, Roland. "Introduction à l'analyse structurale des récits," *Communications* 8 (1966): 1–27; published in English as "Introduction to the Structuralist Analysis of Narrative," trans. Lionel Duisit, *New Literary History* 6 (1975): 237–272.

——. *S/Z.* Trans. Richard Miller New York: Hill & Wang, 1974.

Bayley, John. *The Character of Love: A Study in the Literature of Personality.* New York: Collier [Macmillan], 1963.

Beardsley, Monroe. *Aesthetics: Problems in the Philosophy of Criticism.* New York: Harcourt, Brace & World, 1958.

Bersani, Leo. *A Future for Astyanax: Character and Desire in Literature.* Boston: Little, Brown, 1976.

Bettelheim, Bruno *The Uses of Enchantment: The Meaning and Importance of Fairy Tales.* New York: Vintage Books, 1977.

Bloom, Harold. *The Anxiety of Influence.* New York: Oxford University Press, 1973.

Bradley, A. C. *Shakespearean Tragedy.* Greenwich, Conn.: Fawcett, n.d. Originally published in 1904.

Brandeis, Irma. *The Ladder of Vision: A Study of Dante's "Comedy."* Garden City, N.Y.: Doubleday/Anchor, 1962.

Bremond, Claude. *Logique du récit.* Paris: Seuil, 1973.

Brenner, Charles. *An Elementary Textbook of Psychoanalysis.* Garden City, N.Y.: Doubleday, 1955.

Bullough, Edward. *Aesthetics: Lectures and Essays.* London: Bowes & Bowes, 1957.

Butler, Samuel. *Notebooks.* Cited on title page of Claude C. H. Williamson, ed., *Readings on the Character of Hamlet* (1974).

Chase, Richard. "The Brontës, or Myth Domesticated." *Kenyon Review* 9 (1947): 487–506.

Chatman, Seymour. *Story and Discourse.* Ithaca: Cornell University Press, 1978.

Chevigny, Bell Gale, ed. Introduction to *Twentieth-Century Interpretations: Endgame.* Englewood Cliffs, N.J.: Prentice-Hall, 1969.

Cixous, Hélène. "The Character of 'Character.'" *New Literary History* 5 (1974): 383–400.

Cohn, Dorrit. *Transparent Minds.* Princeton: Princeton University Press, 1978.

Culler, Jonathan. *Flaubert.* Ithaca: Cornell University Press, 1974.

——. *Structuralist Poetics.* Ithaca: Cornell University Press, 1975.

Daleski, H. M. *The Divided Heroine: A Recurrent Pattern in Six English Novels.* New York: Holmes & Meier, 1984.

Danby, John. *Shakespeare's Doctrine of Nature.* London: Faber & Faber, 1962.

Dauber, Antoinette B. "Allegory and Irony in *Othello*." Unpublished essay.

Dearlove, J.E. *Accommodating to Chaos: Samuel Beckett's Nonrelational Art.* Durham, N.C.: Duke University Press, 1982.

Edel, Leon. *Literary Biography.* London: R. Hart-Davis, 1957.

Eliot, T. S. "Tradition and the Individual Talent." In *Selected Essays*. New York: Harcourt, Brace, 1950.

Ewen, Yosef. *Character in Narrative* (in Hebrew). Tel Aviv: Sifriyat Hapoalim, 1980.

Fanger, Donald. *Dostoevsky and Romantic Realism*. Chicago: University of Chicago Press, 1967.

Felperin, Howard Michael. *Shakespearean Representation: Mimesis and Modernity in Elizabethan Tragedy*. Princeton: Princeton University Press, 1977.

Fergusson, Francis. *Dante*. New York: Macmillan, 1966.

——. *The Idea of a Theatre*. Garden City, N.Y.: Doubleday/Anchor, 1953.

Flores, Angel. *Cervantes across the Centuries*. New York: Gordian Press, 1948.

Forster, E. M. *Aspects of the Novel*. New York: Harcourt, Brace, 1927.

Frank, Joseph. *The Widening Gyre: Crisis and Mastery in Modern Literature*. Bloomington: Indiana University Press, 1973.

Freud, Sigmund. *Character and Culture*. Ed. Phillip Rieff. New York: Collier, 1963.

Freund, Elizabeth. "Arachne's Broken Web." In Patricia Parker and Geoffrey Hartman, eds., *Shakespeare and the Question of Theory*. London: Methuen, forthcoming.

Frye, Northrop. *Anatomy of Criticism*. Princeton: Princeton University Press, 1957.

Gardiner, Muriel, ed. *The Wolf Man by the Wolf Man*. New York: Basic Books, 1971.

Gardner, Joseph H. "Dickens, Romance and *McTeague:* A Study in Mutual Interpretation." In Donald Pizer, ed., *McTeague: A Critical Edition*, pp. 361–377. New York: Norton, 1977.

Gass, William H. *Fiction and the Figures of Life*. New York: Knopf, 1970.

Geertz, Clifford. *The Interpretation of Cultures*. New York: Basic Books, 1973.

Genette, Gérard. *Narrative Discourse*. Trans. Jane E. Lewin. Ithaca: Cornell University Press, 1980.

——. "Vraisemblance et motivation." *Communications* 11 (1969).

Gombrich, E. H. "Meditations on a Hobby Horse, or the Roots of Artistic Form." In *Meditations on a Hobby Horse*. London: Phaidon, 1978.

Greenblatt, Stephen. *Renaissance Self-Fashioning: From More to Shakespeare.* Chicago: University of Chicago Press, 1980.

Greimas, Algirdas Julien. *Semantique structurale.* Paris: Larousse, 1966.

Hardison, O.B., and H. Golden, eds. *Aristotle's Poetics.* Englewood Cliffs, N.J., 1968.

Harvey, W. John. *Character and the Novel.* Ithaca: Cornell University Press, 1965.

Hochman, Baruch. "Joyce's *Portrait* as Portrait." *Literary Review* 22 (Fall 1978): 25–55.

———. "Joyce's *Ulysses* and Homer's *Odyssey*." *Scripta Hierosolymitana* 25 (1973): 214–226.

———. *The Test of Character: From the Victorian Novel to the Modern.* Rutherford, N.J.: Fairleigh Dickinson University Press, 1983.

Holland, Norman N. "Fantasy and Defense in Faulkner's 'A Rose for Emily.'" *Hartford Studies in Literature* 4 (1972): 1–35.

———. *5 Readers Reading.* New Haven: Yale University Press, 1977.

———. *Poems in Persons.* New York: Norton, 1975.

Hume, David. *A Treatise of Human Nature,* ed. D. G. C. Macnabb. New York: Collins, n.d.

Ingarden, Roman. *The Literary Work of Art.* Trans. George C. Grabowicz. Evanston, Ill.: Northwestern University Press, 1973. Originally published in 1931.

Iser, Wolfgang. *The Act of Reading.* London: Routledge and Kegan Paul, 1978.

———. "Indeterminacy in the Reader's Response in Prose Fiction." In J. Hillis Miller, ed., *Aspects of Narrative: Selected Papers from the English Institute.* New York: Columbia University Press, 1971.

Jagendorf, Zvi. "All against One in *Troilus and Cressida*." *English* 141 (Autumn 1982): 199–210.

Jakobson, Roman. "The Metaphoric and Metonymic Poles." In Hazard Adams, ed., *Critical Theory since Plato.* pp. 1113–1116. New York: Harcourt Brace Jovanovich, 1971.

James, Henry. *The Art of Fiction.* New York: Oxford University Press, 1948.

———. Preface to *The Portrait of a Lady.* Harmondsworth: Penguin, 1960. Originally published in 1908.

Jameson, Fredric. *The Political Unconscious: Narrative as a Socially Symbolic Act.* Ithaca: Cornell University Press, 1982.

Jones, Ernest. *Hamlet and Oedipus*. Garden City, N.Y.: Doubleday/ Anchor, 1952. Originally published in 1949.

Jones, John. *On Aristotle and Greek Tragedy*. London: Chatto & Windus, 1962.

Kettle, Arnold. *An Introduction to the English Novel*, vol. 1, *Defoe to George Eliot*. New York: Harper Torchbooks, 1965.

Khazoum, Violet. "The Inverted Comedy of *Tristram Shandy*." *Hebrew University Studies in Literature* 7 (Autumn 1979): 139–160.

Knight, Everett. *Theory of the Classical Novel*. London: Routledge & Kegan Paul, 1970.

Knight, G. Wilson. *The Wheel of Fire*. London: Methuen, 1961.

Knights, L. C. *Explorations*. London: Chatto & Windus, 1965.

Kovel, Joel. "Heathcliff's Quest." *Hebrew Studies in Literature* 13 (Spring, 1985).

———. "On Reading *Madame Bovary* Psychoanalytically." *Seminars in Psychiatry* 4 (August 1973).

Krieger, Murray. *Poetic Presence and Illusion*. Baltimore: Johns Hopkins University Press, 1979.

Krook, Dorothea. *The Ordeal of Consciousness in Henry James*. Cambridge: Cambridge University Press, 1967.

Lacan, Jacques. *Écrits I*. Paris: Points, 1966.

Landau, John. "*The Ambassadors:* The Story of the Story." *Hebrew University Studies in Literature* 12 (Spring 1984): 85–115.

Langbaum, Robert. *The Poetry of Experience*. London: Chatto & Windus, 1952.

Lanham, Richard A. *Motives of Eloquence*. New Haven: Yale University Press, 1976.

Lord, Albert B. *The Singer of Tales*. New York: Atheneum, 1973.

Lubbock, Percy. *The Craft of Fiction*. New York: Peter Smith, 1947.

Lukács, Georg. *Studies in European Realism*. New York: Grosset & Dunlap. 1964.

———. *Theory of the Novel*. Cambridge: MIT Press, 1972.

McCarthy, Mary. "Characters in Fiction." *Partisan Review* 28 (1961): 172–194.

Matejka, Ladislav, and Krystyna Pomorska, eds. *Readings in Russian Poetics: Formalist and Structuralist Views*. Cambridge: MIT Press, 1971.

Mead, G. H. *Mind, Self, Society*. Chicago: Yinger, 1934.

Morgann, Maurice. *An Essay on the Dramatic Character of Falstaff* (1777). Excerpted in G. K. Hunter, ed., *Casebook on Henry IV, Parts 1 and 2*. New York: Macmillan, 1970.

Moser, Thomas. "What's the Matter with Emily Jane?" In Moser, ed., *Wuthering Heights: Texts, Sources, Critics*. New York: Harcourt, Brace & World, 1962.

Muir, Edwin. *The Structure of the Novel*. London: Hogarth Press, 1974. First published in 1928.

Nevo, Ruth. *Tragic Form in Shakespeare*. Princeton: Princeton University Press, 1972.

Ortega y Gasset, José. *The Dehumanization of Art; and Notes on the Novel*. Princeton: Princeton University Press, 1948.

O'Toole, John. "Approaches to the Narrative Structure." In Roger Fowler, ed., *Style and Structure in Literature: Essays in the New Stylistics*. Ithaca: Cornell University Press, 1975.

Pearlman, E. "David Copperfield's Dream of Drowning." In Leonard Tennenhouse, ed., *The Practice of Psychoanalytic Criticism*. Detroit: Wayne State University Press, 1976.

Perry, Menakhem. "Literary Dynamics: How the Order of a Text Creates Its Meanings (with an Analysis of Faulkner's 'A Rose for Emily')." *Poetics Today* 1 (1979): 35–64, 311–361.

Price, Martin. "The Irrelevant Detail and the Emergence of Form." In J. Hillis Miller, ed., *Aspects of Narrative: Selected Papers from the English Institute*. New York: Columbia University Press, 1971.

——. "The Other Self: Thoughts about Character in the Novel." In Maynard Mack and Ian Gregor, eds., *Imagined Worlds*. London: Methuen, 1968.

Prince, Gerald. *A Grammar of Stories*. The Hague: Mouton, 1973.

Propp, Vladimir. *Morphology of the Folk Tale*. Austin: University of Texas Press, 1977.

Rank, Otto. *The Double: A Psychoanalytic Study*. Trans. Harry Tucker, Jr. Chapel Hill: University of North Carolina Press, 1971.

Reich, Wilhelm. *Character Analysis*. 3d ed. Trans. Vincent E. Carafagno. New York: Farrar, Straus & Giroux, 1972.

Rickword, C. H. "A Note on Fiction." In F. R. Leavis, ed., *Toward a Standard of Criticism*. London, 1931.

Rimmon, Shlomith. *The Concept of Ambiguity: The Example of Henry James*. Chicago: University of Chicago Press, 1977.

Rimmon-Kenan, Shlomith. *Narrative Fiction*. London: Methuen, 1983.

Robbe-Grillet, Alain. *For a New Novel*. Trans. Richard Howard. New York: Grove Press, 1965.

Romano, John. *Dickens and Reality*. New York: Columbia University Press, 1978.

Ron, Moshe. "Autobiographical Narration and Formal Closure in *Great Expectations*." *Hebrew University Studies in Literature* 5 (Spring 1977): 37–66.

Rorty, Amelie Oxenhandler, ed. *The Identities of Persons*. Berkeley: University of California Press, 1976.

Rutherford, John. "Galdós 'El amigo manso.'" In Roger Fowler, ed., *Style and Structure in Literature: Essays in the New Stylistics*. Ithaca: Cornell University Press, 1975.

Rymer, Thomas. *Critical Works*. Ed. C. A. Zimansky. New Haven: Yale University Press, 1956.

Sandbank, Shimon. "Myth and Anti-myth in Kafka" (in Hebrew). In *Kafka Symposium*. Tel Aviv: Sifriyat Hapoalim, 1982.

Santayana, George. *Three Philosophical Poets*. New York: Cooper Square, 1970.

Scholes, Robert, and Robert Kellogg. *The Nature of Narrative*. New York: Oxford University Press, 1968.

Skura, Meredith Anne. *The Literary Use of the Psychoanalytic Process*. New Haven: Yale University Press, 1981.

Snell, Bruno. *The Discovery of the Mind*. Trans. T. G. Rosenmeyer. New York: Harper & Row, 1960.

Sternberg, Meir, and Menakhem Perry. "The King through Ironic Eyes: The Narrator's Devices in the Biblical Story of David and Bathsheba and Two Excursuses on the Theory of the Narrative Text" (in Hebrew). *HaSifrut* 1 (1968): 263–292.

Stoll, E. E. *Art and Artifice in Shakespeare*. New York: Barnes & Noble, 1951.

Suleiman, Susan R. "Varieties of Audience-Oriented Criticism." Introduction to S. R. Suleiman and I. Crosman, eds., *The Reader in the Text: Essays on Audience and Interpretation*. Princeton: Princeton University Press, 1980.

Tanner, Tony. *City of Words: American Fiction, 1950–1970*. London: Jonathan Cape, 1971.

Telford, Kenneth A. *Aristotle's Poetics: Translation and Analysis*. Chicago: Henry Regnery, 1961.

Todorov, Tzvetan. *Grammaire du "Décameron."* The Hague: Mouton, 1969.

——. "Narrative Men." In Todorov, *The Poetics of Prose*, trans. Richard Howard. Ithaca: Cornell University Press, 1977.

Toker, Leona. "A Nabokovian Character in Conrad's *Nostromo*."

Tolstoy, Leo. "Shakespeare and the Drama." In Tolstoy, *Recollections and Essays*, trans. Aylmer Maude. London: Oxford University Press, 1937.

Tomashevsky, Boris. "Thematics." In Lee T. Lemon and Marion J. Reis, eds., *Russian Formalist Criticism: Four Essays*. Lincoln: University of Nebraska Press, 1965.

Van Ghent, Dorothy. *The English Novel: Form and Function*. New York: Holt, Rinehart & Winston, 1953.

Watt, Ian. *The Rise of the Novel*. Berkeley: University of California Press, 1967.

Weinsheimer, Joel. "Theory of Character: *Emma*." *Poetics Today* 1 (Autumn 1979): 185–211.

Weinstein, Arnold. *Fictions of the Self: 1550–1800*. Princeton: Princeton University Press, 1981.

Wilson, John Dover. *What Happens in "Hamlet."* Cambridge: Cambridge University Press, 1967.

Wilson, Rawdon. "The Bright Chimera: Character as a Literary Term." *Critical Inquiry* 5 (1979): 725–749.

——. "On Character: A Reply to Martin Price." *Critical Inquiry* 2 Autumn (1975): 191–198.

Wolterstorff, Nicholas. "Characters and Their Names." *Poetics* 8 (1979): 101–127.

——. "Worlds of Works of Art." *Journal of Aesthetics and Art History* 35 (Winter 1976): 121–137.

Woolf, Virginia. "Character in Fiction" *Criterion* 2 (July 1924): 409–430.

——. "David Copperfield." *The Nation*, August 22, 1925, reprinted in Stephen Wall, ed., *Charles Dickens: A Critical Anthology*, pp. 273–276. Harmondsworth: Penguin, 1970.

Index

Characters, titles, and authors are listed separately.

Index

Index

Index

Library of Congress Cataloging in Publication Data

Hochman, Baruch, 1930–
    Character in literature.

    Bibliography: p.
    Includes index.
    1. Characters and characteristics in literature. I. Title.
PN56.4H63   1985   809'.927   84–45809
ISBN 0–8014–1787–2 (alk. paper)